Henry Stephens Salt, William Godwin

Godwin's Political Justice

A Reprint from the Essay on Property

Henry Stephens Salt, William Godwin

Godwin's Political Justice
A Reprint from the Essay on Property

ISBN/EAN: 9783337072629

Printed in Europe, USA, Canada, Australia, Japan

Cover: Foto ©Suzi / pixelio.de

More available books at **www.hansebooks.com**

CONTENTS.

SOCIAL SCIENCE SERIES

Each 2s. 6d.

SWAN SONNENSCHEIN & CO., LONDON.

GODWIN'S "POLITICAL JUSTICE."

A Reprint of the Essay on Property.

INTRODUCTORY NOTE.

IT is now close on a hundred years since the world was startled by the appearance of a book which, both by the significance of its title and the strangeness of its conclusions, was well calculated to arrest the attention—friendly or hostile, as the case might be—of every reader into whose hands it might fall. It is difficult for us, who live in a less speculative and sanguine age, to realize the keen interest which attached to the publication, in 1793, of William Godwin's *Political Justice*, at a crisis when men's minds were strung to a high pitch of expectant enthusiasm by the thrill of excitement of which the French Revolution was the cause; but the testimony of contemporary authors, whatever their personal sympathies might be, is explicit on this point. "No work in our time," says Hazlitt, "gave such a blow to the philosophical mind of the country as Godwin's celebrated *Enquiry concerning Political Justice.* Tom Paine was considered for the time as a Tom Fool to him; Paley an old woman; Edmund Burke a flashy sophist. Truth, moral truth, it was supposed, had here taken up its abode, and these were the oracles of thought." "Burn your books of chemistry," was Wordsworth's advice to a student, "and read Godwin on Necessity." "Faulty as it is in many parts," wrote Southey, "there is a mass of truth in it that must make every man think." We are told by De Quincey that Godwin's book "carried one single shock into the bosom of English society, fearful but momentary." "In the quarto," he adds,—"that is, the original edition of his *Political Justice*,—Mr. Godwin advanced against thrones and dominations, powers and principalities, with the air of some Titan slinger or monomachist from Thebes and Troy, saying, 'Come hither, ye wretches, that I may give your flesh to the fowls of the air.'"

It might well have been expected, in an age when government prosecutions were so rife, that the powers thus challenged would have retaliated with full severity on their venturesome opponent. It is said that *Political Justice* owed its immunity from prosecution solely to the fact that it appeared in an expensive form; for when the question was discussed in the Privy Council, it was remarked by Pitt that "a three-

guinea book could never do much harm among those
who had not three shillings to spare." In this respect
Pitt's judgment seems to have been less shrewd than
might be supposed, for it is recorded that *Political
Justice* "became so popular that the poorest mechanics
were known to club subscriptions for its purchase, and
thus it was directed to mine and eat away contentment
from a nation's roots."[1] Godwin himself indirectly
corroborates this statement. " I had a numerous
audience," he says, " of all classes, of every age, and
of every sex. The young and the fair did not feel
deterred from consulting my pages."

The author who rose into this sudden notoriety as
the advocate of the most revolutionary views was the
descendant on both sides of respectable middle-class
families, his father being a Dissenting minister at
Wisbeach, in Cambridgeshire, in which place William
Godwin was born, March 3rd, 1756. He was brought
up in an atmosphere of ultra-Calvinistic doctrines as
a follower of Sandeman, "a celebrated north country
apostle," as Godwin expresses it, " who, after Calvin
had damned ninety-nine in a hundred of mankind, con-
trived a scheme for damning ninety-nine in a hundred
of the followers of Calvin." Among the boy's earliest
books were the *Pilgrim's Progress* and the *Pious Deaths
of many Godly Children;* and so serious was his tem-

[1] *Gentleman's Magazine,* June, 1836.

perament, that it was his practice, when occasion permitted, to discourse to his school-fellows on the congenial subject of sin and damnation. From the first, the leading traits of his character were an indefatigable zeal in the search for truth, and a calm, intellectual gravity, underlaid, and at times dominated, by an insatiable self-esteem. After receiving his education at Norwich and Hoxton College, he undertook and discharged the duties of a Nonconformist minister at Stowmarket, and other places, for a period of about eight years, publishing, in 1784, a volume of six sermons, under the title of *Sketches of History*, in which, while in the main writing as an orthodox Calvinist, he advanced the significant and characteristic proposition that "God himself has no right to be a tyrant."

In a few years from this time his religious faith, which had already been shaken by a study of the French philosophers, underwent a complete change, and from 1787 onward he gave up the ministry, to become an avowed and uncompromising advocate of the principles of free thought. Urged partly by the need of finding a livelihood,—for his means were very limited,—partly by a natural inclination to a literary profession, he settled in London, where he became acquainted with Sheridan, Canning, Holcroft, and other men of note, and won some distinction as a vigorous exponent of advanced political opinion. He wrote articles for the *Political Herald*, contributed a sketch of English History to the *New Annual Register*, and published, in 1788, his first serious attempt in literature—a *Life of Lord Chatham*. It was during this period that he conceived and formulated the theories which subsequently found expression in *Political Justice*—a line of thought to which he was especially stimulated by his intercourse with Holcroft. In 1791 we find the project assuming definite shape. " This year," writes Godwin in his autobiographical notes,[1] " was the main crisis of my life. I suggested to Robinson the bookseller the idea of composing a treatise on Political Principles, and he agreed to aid me in executing it. In the first fervour of my enthusiasm, I entertained the vain imagination of ' hewing a stone from the rock,' which, by its inherent energy and weight, should overbear and annihilate all opposition, and place the principles of politics on an immovable basis." The work, which was executed with much slowness and deliberation, was published in February, 1793.

Political Justice, as the name implies, is essentially a *moral* treatise, concerning " the adoption of any principle of morality and truth into the practice of a community." Starting with the assumption that " we bring into the world with us no innate principles," and that " the moral qualities of men are the produce

---

[1] *Life of William Godwin.* By C. Kegan Paul.

of the impressions made upon them," Godwin pro-
ceeded to argue that, by the gradual improvement of
human surroundings and institutions, vice and misery
may be ultimately extirpated from the world.   This
perfectibility of man in the future (a theory which had
already been advanced by Priestley in his *First Principles of Government*), was not based by Godwin, as is
sometimes supposed, on the contingency of a sudden
and supernatural change in human nature, but rather
on a study of the improvements already effected in
the past.   While admitting that both individuals
and nations are powerfully affected by the influence
of climate, heredity, and other physical causes, he yet
maintains that Reason is in the main omnipotent, and
that where the truth is clearly enunciated it must
finally prevail; the three most effective methods of
reform being Literature, Education, and that notion
of Political Justice which it was his special purpose
to inculcate.[1]

Justice is defined as "a rule of conduct originat-
ing in the connection of one percipient being with
another;" its object is the *general* good, which must
take precedence of all considerations of a private or
personal nature.   In dealing with this point, Godwin
was led by his passion for logical consistency into a
denial of the excellence of the domestic affections, as

---

[1] *Political Justice*, original edition, Book i.

partialities which are incompatible with a strict regard
for the interests of the community; but the more para-
doxical arguments of this portion of his treatise
were afterwards withdrawn by him. The doctrine of
" rights," whether belonging to the individual or
society, in the sense of "a full and complete power of
either doing a thing or omitting it, without liability
to animadversion or censure," is entirely contraverted,
every member of the community being held morally
accountable for his own actions, and possessing in his
turn "a diploma constituting him inquisitor-general of
the moral conduct of his neighbours." This brings
us to the subject of the duty (not "right") of private judgment—one of the most important and most
strongly emphasized of all Godwin's contentions. "To
a rational being," he asserts, " there can be but one
rule of conduct—justice ; and one mode of ascertaining
that rule—the exercise of the understanding." In
other words, he advocates an absolute intellectual
individualism, subject only to the moral censorship of
society.[1]

From the adoption of these anarchist principles he
necessarily proceeds to the condemnation of all systems
of government as at the best a temporary expedient
and makeshift. " Since government," he says, " even
in its best state is an evil, the object principally to be

[1] Book ii.

aimed at is that we should have as little of it as the
general peace of human society will permit,"—a sentiment which, in one form or another, repeatedly occurs
in the pages of *Political Justice*. But he is careful to
add, in accordance with the dictates of his slow and
cautious temperament, that all violent resistance is
earnestly to be deprecated, and that a revolution, to
be successful, must be effected not by force, but by
argument and persuasion, and consist in a genuine
change of character and conviction ; we must " carefully distinguish between informing the people and
inflaming them."   To such a length did Godwin
carry his dread of popular tumult, that he objects
even to Political Associations as likely to retard the
cause of moral progress.   He maintains that the
spread of intellectual enlightenment is the great engine
of liberty ; and that the benevolence which prompts
men to consult the welfare of their fellows originates
in a higher motive than self-love.   " Neither philosophy," he says, " nor morality, nor politics, will ever
show like themselves, till man shall be acknowledged
for what he really is—a being capable of justice, virtue, and benevolence."   The doctrine of Necessity is
frankly and fully accepted by Godwin as corroborat-
ing rather than weakening the general force of his
scheme.   A belief in this doctrine, he argues, so far
from paralyzing moral action, should have a contrary
result, for " the more certain the connection between

effects and causes, the more cheerfulness should I feel in yielding to painful and laborious employments."[1]

In the second volume of *Political Justice* we have the application of these abstract moral principles to various existing institutions. Monarchy and aristocracy are considered and criticised in all their bearings; while all religious establishments, tests, oaths, libel laws, and other obstacles to the development of individual liberty, are declared to be objectionable. It is curious to note that the introduction of the ballot at parliamentary elections (an assembly of delegates for common deliberation is regarded by Godwin as the least blameworthy form of government) is deprecated as teaching us "to draw a veil of concealment over the performance of our duty." Even National Education is rejected by this uncompromising individualist, as likely to produce too much permanence and uniformity of thought.[2]

To the employment of a Penal Code and coercion of any violent kind Godwin, both as a necessarian and a philanthropist, offers the most strenuous opposition. Punishment, he maintains, can only be justified by the correction of the offender. "It cannot be just that we should inflict suffering on any man, except so far as it tends to good." He points out the impossibility of rightly estimating the motives of a "criminal,"

---

[1] Books iii. and iv.   [2] Books v. and vi.

since every man's criterion of duty must lie in the exercise of his private judgment. "How few," he exclaims, "are the trials which an humane and a just man can read, terminating in a verdict of guilty, without feeling an incontrollable repugnance against the verdict."

The concluding portion of Godwin's *Enquiry*, of which a reprint is now offered to the public, is devoted to the momentous question of Property, which he declares to be "the key-stone that completes the fabric of political justice." It will be seen that, keeping justice in view as the sole criterion of conduct, he insists that all possessions are in strict equity a common stock, from which all men are entitled to draw according to their own needs and those of their fellow-citizens; and that he sets forth and emphasizes the evils of the present system of competition, which results in the demoralization of rich and poor alike. This essay on *Property* is perhaps the most interesting and characteristic of all Godwin's writings, containing as it does an epitome of his social doctrines, and exhibiting him both in the stronger and the weaker aspects of his work—the ardent communist, whose creed it is that a loaf of bread belongs "to him who most wants it;" the equally ardent individualist, who, in spite of his communism, would minimise co-operation as at best a necessary evil; the enthusiastic dreamer, whose faith in human perfectibility, and in

the regenerating power of the mind, points to an
ultimate triumph over every physical limitation. It
should be remembered by those who blame Godwin
for ignoring the intermediate steps that must be
laboriously taken before man can even approach this
state of perfection, that he was avowedly writing of
an ideal and abstract condition, and that the over-
sanguine mood which occasionally prompted him to
absurd and extravagant statements was one which he
shared with Fourier, Owen, and other thinkers of his
time. It is easy to ridicule and caricature such
speculations by applying, or rather misapplying, the
criticism of to-day to views which have reference
solely to a future period; but it is well, nevertheless,
that our thoughts should be sometimes directed towards this final and ultimate goal of human aspirations.

The strength of Godwin's *Political Justice* consists
in its moral earnestness: it is an appeal from the
fetters of restrictive institutions to the higher and
nobler elements in human nature. If eclectic rather
than original in the opinions it embodies (and Godwin fully acknowledges his various debt to Hume,
Locke, Priestley, Rousseau, and other writers), it
may, nevertheless, claim originality in the new force
which these opinions acquired when collected, re-
stated, emphasized, and made to converge towards one
unmistakable conclusion, by that intellectual calmness
and that perspicuity of language which were Godwin's

peculiar characteristics. Its weakness lies in the fact that its author, carried too far perhaps by the ambition and enthusiasm of the moment, attempted to give the appearance of complete logical consistency and scientific precision to a work which is based primarily on humane sentiment, and does not admit of being constructed into an irrefragable "system," however powerfully it may influence a certain class of mind. In his preface to a later volume,[1] Godwin himself recognised the danger that attends such *a priori* reasoning as he had adopted in *Political Justice* by "laying down one or two simple principles which seem scarcely to be exposed to the hazard of reputation, and then developing them, applying them to a number of points, and following them into a variety of inferences." In such a process, he adds, "a mistake at the commencement is fatal;" and the critics have not been lacking who have contended that Godwin made this mistake. As far, then, as it was intended to be a positive system, which should "overbear and annihilate all opposition," *Political Justice* must be adjudged to have been a failure; but, regarded as a treatise on morals, it not only created a deep impression at the time, but will always appeal powerfully to those readers who have any natural tendency to sympathise with its author's ideals. It is a grave, lucid, and

---

[1] *The Enquirer,* 1797.

forcible presentment of the arguments in favour of the reorganization of society on a simpler basis, with benevolence instead of authority as its guiding principle ; and it avowedly treats less of what is immediately practicable than of what is ultimately desirable— a fact which is of itself an answer to a good deal of the irrelevant criticism of which Godwin has been the mark.

That Godwin, writing before the age of Darwinian discovery, should greatly underrate the vast scope and power of hereditary instincts, was of course inevitable ; nor could he, any more than the other philosophic radicals of his day, grasp the significance of those economic changes which were already replacing individual by collective industry, and rendering a policy of governmental *laisser faire* intolerable. In these respects he shared the disabilities of those among whom he lived. But he was not guilty of the gross absurdities which some of his critics—misunderstanding his meaning through lack of sympathy with the spirit in which he wrote—are too apt to attribute to him. It has been said that he " believes as firmly as any Christian in the speedy revelation of a New Jerusalem—four-square and perfect in its plan "[1]— a mere caricature this, of the theory of perfectibility, which, as has already been stated, does not portend

[1] Leslie Stephen's *English Thought of the Eighteenth Century.*

a miraculous perfection, but is simply the belief that an observation of human efforts in years past justifies us in anticipating an unlimited progress in years to come. Godwin himself, so far from being animated, as some have supposed, by an unscientific prejudice against the historical method, was himself a successful student and writer of history. "History," he tells us, "was a study to which I felt a peculiar vocation." "I trust that none of my readers," he elsewhere remarks, [1] "will be erroneous enough to consider the vivid recollection of things past as hostile to that tone of spirit which should aspire to the boldest improvements in the future."

Equally false is the idea that Godwin in his tirade against kings, priests, and tyrants, was unaware of the consideration (gravely pointed out by his critics) that government cannot be regarded as the external cause of political evil, since it must itself be an effect of some internal trait in human nature. This objection not only is not overlooked by Godwin, but is met and answered by anticipation, his charge against government being not that it introduced evil where none existed before, but that it fosters and strengthens it by "giving substance and permanence to our errors." As to the exaggerated antipathy to kings and priests, as the prime enemies of the human race, with which

---

[1] Preface to *Essay on Sepulchres*, 1809.

he is often accredited, it is sufficient to point out that he declares the miseries which are caused by the unequal distribution of property to be worse than those resulting from any other source whatsoever.[1] Finally, the equality of men, on which he of course insists, is not based on the fabulous notion (which some learned persons now-a-days think it worth their while to demolish), that men are born equal in mental and physical endowments, but on the fact that " we are partakers of a common nature, and the same causes that contribute to the benefit of one contribute to the benefit of another."

In the second edition of his book, which appeared in 1796, Godwin modified some of the views which were so strongly and plainly expressed in the original quarto. "In this collapse of a tense excitement," says De Quincey, "I myself find the true reason for the utter extinction of the *Political Justice,* and of its author considered as a philosopher." It seems more probable, however, that the decrease of public interest in Godwin's work was due to the subsidence of that political agitation which first brought it into note. "Books, as well as men," says Mackintosh, "are subject to what is called fortune. The same circumstances which favoured the sudden popularity of *Political Justice* have since unduly depressed its

---

[1] See p. 47.

reputation. The moment for doing full and exact justice will come."

The seven years that followed the publication of *Political Justice* saw Godwin in the prime of his powers and at the zenith of his fame. While the spirit of enthusiasm was still strong in his mind, he wrote his most successful novel, *Caleb Williams,* designed to be "a general review of the modes of domestic despotism, by which man becomes the destroyer of man," in which aspect it may be regarded as the pendant and complement of the preceding work. The main subject of the story is the persecution undergone by Caleb Williams, a raw youth, full of natural inquisitiveness and a mild yet indomitable pertinacity (somewhat suggestive of Godwin himself), at the hands of his master Falkland, into whose guilty secret he has been rash and injudicious enough to pry. The penalties attendant on simplicity and love of knowledge, when they offend the prejudices of the wealthy and powerful, are thus incidentally illustrated; while the character of Falkland, a courtly and high-minded gentleman, who, to avenge a gross insult, had been tempted, years before, into the commission of a terrible crime, gave Godwin the opportunity of preaching an eloquent sermon on a favourite text— the iniquity of that "code of honour" which would seek satisfaction for a real or supposed injury in any other way than by argument and expostulation.

Caleb Williams, which was published in 1794, attained a wider popularity than any of Godwin's other works, doubtless because its didactic purpose is concealed— and concealed with more skill than one would have expected from so serious a writer—under the form of a narrative. "It is the cream of his mind," says Allan Cunningham; "the rest are the skimmed milk." The encomiums passed on this novel by Sir T. N. Talfourd, Gilfillan, and other contemporaries of Godwin, were somewhat extravagant; but the book is a powerful and remarkable one, and less read at the present time than its merits would make us expect.

In this same year, 1794, Godwin wrote several letters to the *Morning Chronicle* on the subject of the state trials by which the Government was then seeking to destroy some of the more prominent of the advocates of reform; and it was in great measure owing to his crushing answer to the charge of Chief Justice Eyre that a verdict of acquittal was returned in favour of the twelve men who were put on their trial in October, among whom were Holcroft, Horne Tooke, and others of Godwin's friends. "The feeling of triumph among the friends of liberty," says Mrs. Shelley, "was universal. Godwin never forgot the delightful sensations he then experienced; it was his honest boast, and most grateful recollection, that he had contributed to the glorious result by his letter to Chief Justice Eyre."

c

The Enquirer, a volume of essays published in 1797, is said by Gilfillan to be "made up of orts and fragments which were over from the great feast of the *Enquiry*." It is, however, as Godwin indicates in his Preface, an approach on Truth from another side than that of *Political Justice*, being based on *a posteriori* instead of *a priori* reasoning, and on an "incessant recurrence to experiment and actual observation." Its author confesses that he did not escape the contagion of the French Revolution, but was too impatient and impetuous in certain passages of his earlier work; he therefore wishes to descend into "the humbler walks of private life," and to study in *The Enquirer* points which had been overlooked in *Political Justice*. The essay, however, which treats of "Riches and Poverty," was corroborative, in the main, of the opinions already expressed by Godwin on the subject of property.

At this time, as indeed during the greater part of his life, Godwin's circle of acquaintances was very wide. The four friends by whom he was most strongly influenced in his intellectual development were, as he himself records, Joseph Fawcet, Thomas Holcroft, George Dyson, and S. T. Coleridge. With Holcroft and Coleridge in particular he was on terms of affectionate intimacy. Charles Lamb, Mackintosh, Horne Tooke, Dr. Parr, Mrs. Inchbald, were also among Godwin's friends, and he was more or less acquainted with most of the eminent men of that time. "Let me tell you, Godwin," wrote Coleridge in a letter of 1800, "that four such men as you, I, Davy, and Wordsworth, do not meet together in one house every day of the year—I mean four men so distinct with so many sympathies."

Godwin's habits were extremely simple and methodical, his mode of living frugal and unpretending, as befitted a man of his calm, thoughtful, unimpassioned temperament. His appearance may best be judged from the portrait by Northcote (most of the written accounts that have been preserved refer to a later period of his life), which shows us a strong, stern countenance, full of intellectual gravity and determination, with lofty, massive brow, earnest eyes, large nose, and firmly chiselled mouth. His nose, if we may trust Southey's humorous and not altogether friendly description, was the least prepossessing of his features. "As for Godwin," he wrote in 1797, "he has large noble eyes, and a nose—oh, most abominable nose! Language is not vituperatious enough to describe the effect of its downward elongation." Godwin, in spite of his unemotional disposition, was an ardent, and at times even a jealous friend. "Except the one great passion of his life," says his biographer,[1] "friendship stood to him in the place of

---

[1] *William Godwin, his Friends and Contemporaries.* By C. Kegan Paul.

passion, as morality was to him in the place of devo-
tion. All the jealousies, misunderstandings, wounded
feelings, and the like, which some men experience in
their love affairs, Godwin suffered in his relations
with his friends. And his relations with women were
for the most part the same as those with men." His
influence over youths, many of whom came to him for
consultation and advice, was one of his most remarkable gifts; and this influence seems in every case to
have been exercised with kindliness and discretion.

The "one great passion of his life" was of course
his love for the celebrated Mary Wollstonecraft, then
known as Mrs. Imlay, authoress of the *Vindication of
the Rights of Woman*, to whom he was married in the
early part of 1797. "I think you the most extraordinary married pair in existence," wrote Holcroft to
Godwin, when informed of the marriage; and the
story of their wedded life, so phlegmatic in its out-
ward appearance, so tender in its inner reality, is
certainly one of the strangest on record. By the
death of Mary Wollstonecraft in the autumn of 1797,
at the birth of the daughter who was afterwards Mrs.
Shelley, Godwin was once more left alone; and to this
bereavement may perhaps be traced many of the
troubles that beset his later life. The year after his
wife's death he edited her posthumous works, and
wrote a biographical memoir of her brief but chequered
career. In his novel *St. Leon*, published in 1799, the

character of Marguerite is in several respects a sketch from that of Mary Wollstonecraft, whose influence may also be seen in Godwin's change of attitude towards those domestic ties, the "affections and charities of private life," as he calls them, of which he had spoken disparagingly in *Political Justice.* "For more than four years," he says in his Preface to *St. Leon,* "I have been anxious for opportunity and leisure to modify some of the earlier chapters of that work (*Political Justice*) in conformity to the sentiments inculcated in this."

Had Godwin died at the same time as Mary Wollstonecraft, it is probable that his fame would have stood far higher than it now does with posterity; for there has seldom been a more remarkable instance of a life in which the beginning was signalized by the best of a man's character, and the conclusion by the worst. It has been well observed that Godwin "*lived* in the eighteenth, and only *survived* in the nineteenth century;"[1] and certainly his long life of eighty years may furnish an illustration of the Greek proverb that "the half is greater than the whole." The precise turning point in his career—as far as it is possible to assign an exact date to a general deterioration which affected his fortune and writings alike—was the failure, in 1800, of an ill-starred drama, *Antonio,* on

[1] Leslie Stephen, *Fortnightly Review*, October, 1876.

which he had been rash enough to risk his interests
and his hopes. From that time onward we see him
rather as the needy bookmaker than the disinterested
moralist and man of letters; and the repellent traits
of his character, the egoism and sophistry that had
been latent or less observable in his earlier years,
were now more and more developed and accentuated.
His second marriage, which took place in 1801 (having been preceded by two or three unsuccessful court-
ships), was not altogether a happy one, Mrs. Clairmont,
the widow to whom he allied himself, being a woman
of a strong imperious disposition, which did not conduce to the tranquillity of a philosopher's household;
while the bookselling business, which he undertook
in 1805 and carried on for twenty years, first in
Hanway Street and then in Skinner Street, Holborn,
involved him in a hard, discouraging struggle, beginning in difficulties and ending in complete failure.
It was under the stress of this unlucky commercial
enterprise that Godwin gave way to that demoralizing
habit of borrowing money from every one with whom
he came in contact—friend, acquaintance, or stranger
—with which his name is so largely and dishonourably
associated.[1]   It is only just, however, to note that he

---

[1] In Henry Crabb Robinson's *Diary* for 1812 there is recorded an occasion when Godwin met his match in this
practice of borrowing. "Godwin and Rough met at this
party for the first time. The very next day Godwin called on

was himself open-handed enough when he chanced to have the means of relieving the distress of others, and his biographer records several instances of his " large and self-denying charity, extending to most distant and unexpected quarters."

During these years of misfortune and decay, Godwin still maintained his friendship with Coleridge, Lamb, Holcroft, Curran, Grattan, Horne Tooke, and others, whose acquaintance he had made in happier days; though the number of his friends was now beginning to be thinned by death, and some few of them had become estranged through increasing differences of opinion. That he had also many enemies was due, not to any personal animosity on his part—a fault from which he was singularly free—but to the polemical nature of his writings and the revolutionary opinions of which he was regarded as the exponent. " He had courage of no ordinary kind," says one of his contemporaries, " and needed it all to sustain the reaction of prodigious popularity; every species of attack, from the sun-shafts of Burke, Mackintosh, and

---

me to say how much he liked Rough, adding, ' By the bye, do you think he would lend me £50 just now, as I am in want of a little money?' He had not left me an hour before Rough came in with a like question. He wanted a bill discounted, and asked whether I thought Godwin would do it for him. The habit of both was so well known that some persons were afraid to invite them, lest it should lead to an application for a loan from some friend who chanced to be present."

Hall, to the reptile calumnies of meaner assailants, and a perpetual struggle with narrow circumstances." "I am a man of no fortune or consequence in my country," wrote Godwin himself in 1809;[1] "I am the adherent of no party; I have passed the greater part of my life in solitude and retirement; there are numbers of men who overflow with gall and prejudice against me—God bless them!"

There was one faculty of Godwin's prime which did not desert him in later life—that of attracting and strongly influencing youths of ardent spirit. Of those who were thus led to sit at the feet of the revolutionary prophet, the poet Shelley, afterwards his son-in-law, was the most illustrious example. How great was Shelley's debt to Godwin may be learnt by a study of their respective masterpieces—*Prometheus Unbound* is the poetical and idealized counterpart of *Political Justice*. It is a striking proof of the extent to which Godwin's popularity had waned in the early years of this century, that Shelley, writing to him for the first time in 1811, confesses that he had recently learnt with surprise that Godwin was still living; in his own words, that he had "enrolled his name on the list of the honourable dead." And, in a sense, Shelley's supposition was not so entirely unfounded. The true Godwin, the stern, self-denying

---

[1] Preface to *Essay on Sepulchres*.

reformer, was indeed no more; but in his place was the impecunious bookseller of Skinner Street (" that which was Godwin," Shelley calls him in the " Letter to Maria Gisborne "), whose " implacable exactions " and " boundless and plausible sophistry " were destined to become but too well known to his much-enduring son-in-law.

Godwin's personal appearance, no less than his character, had undergone a great change. " In person," wrote one who knew him, [1] " he was remarkably sedate and solemn, resembling in dress and manner a Dissenting minister rather than the advocate of free thought in all things—religious, moral, social, and intellectual; he was short and stout, his clothes loosely and carelessly put on, and usually old and worn; his hands were generally in his pockets; he had a remarkably large bald head, and a weak voice; seeming generally half asleep when he walked, and even when he talked. Few who saw this man of calm exterior, quiet manners, and inexpressive features, could have believed him to have originated three romances, *Falkland, Caleb Williams,* and *St. Leon,* not yet forgotten because of their terrible excitements; and the work, *Political Justice,* which for a time created a sensation that was a fear in every state of Europe." A more favourable description is that

---

[1] S. C. Hall, *Memories of Great Men,* London, 1871.

given by Harriet Martineau, who made Godwin's acquaintance as late as 1833. "I looked upon him," she says, "as a curious monument of a bygone state of society; and there was still a good deal that was interesting in him. His fine head was striking, and his countenance remarkable." She adds that the portrait which appeared in *Fraser's Magazine*, [1] where Godwin was represented as a small, bent old man, in long tail-coat and immense top-hat, was a malicious caricature, from which it was impossible to form a true estimate of his features.

In 1822, Godwin's bookselling and publishing business had ended in complete bankruptcy, and during the last fourteen years of his life he supported himself by literary work; the presence of his daughter, Mary Shelley, who had now returned from Italy after her husband's death, being a great help and encouragement. Of his later writings, the only one of importance was the answer to Malthus, published in 1820, which has been described as "the first action in the long warfare between the political economists and the various prophets of Utopia," though it may well be doubted if Godwin was the combatant who was "nowhere" in this controversy. The *Life of Chaucer* (1803) is marred by its extraordinary diffuseness, a very slender amount of material being worked up into

---

[1] October, 1834.

two bulky quarto volumes, which drew from Sir Walter Scott the observation that Godwin's method was "hooking in the description and history of everything that existed upon earth at the same time with Chaucer." [1] The *Essay on Sepulchres* (1809) is a brief and pleasantly written proposal "for erecting some memorial of the illustrious dead in all ages on the spot where their remains have been interred." The last work on which Godwin was engaged was the series of essays entitled by him "The Genius of Christianity Unveiled," which, however, did not see the light until 1873, when it appeared under the cautiously indefinite title of *Essays hitherto Unpublished.*

In 1833, Godwin's friends, who had more than once raised subscriptions for his assistance, obtained for him the post of Yeoman Usher of the Exchequer, with residence in New Palace Yard, in the possession of which sinecure he spent the short remainder of his life. Thus were Society and Government triumphantly avenged for the insult offered them forty years previously in *Political Justice;* and it is curious to note that among the many subjects touched on in that work the question of Salaries had not been overlooked by Godwin. "How humiliating," he said, "will it be to the functionary himself, amidst the complication

---

[1] *Edinburgh Review,* iii.

and subtlety of motives, to doubt whether the salary
were not one of his inducements to the acceptance of
the office!" " *Sunt lacrymæ rerum;*" it is a tragedy
of a lifetime on which it would be cruel to dwell;
but it may at least be said in Godwin's favour, that
had he devoted his great powers to the cause of
oppression instead of that of liberty, he would have
ended his days in some far more luxurious sinecure
than his residence in New Palace Yard. " Went to
tea at the Godwins' little dwelling under the roof
of the Houses of Parliament," writes Harriet Martineau in 1834. " Godwin had a small office there, with
a salary, a dwelling, and coals and candle; and very
comfortable he seemed there, with his old wife to take
care of him." It was here that Godwin died on April
7th, 1836, at the age of eighty years. He was buried
in Old Saint Pancras churchyard, by the side of Mary
Wollstonecraft; but in 1851, when this spot was
broken up by the intrusion of the railway, their remains were transferred to the churchyard at Bourne-
mouth, where their daughter, Mary Shelley, had
already been laid to rest.

Godwin's character was a strange mixture of
strength and irresolution, candour and sophistry,
generosity and meanness. A most daring speculator,
even in that age of unlimited theorizing, and gifted
to a remarkable degree with the faculty of patiently
following out his inquiries to their logical conclusion,

he was yet one of the most cautious and timorous of men in conversation and social intercourse. "I am bold and adventurous in opinions," he wrote in an autobiographical fragment—"not in life; it is impossible that a man with my diffidence and embarrassment should be. This, and perhaps only this, renders me often cold, uninviting, and unconciliating in society." His strong didactic tendency, which was unrelieved by any sense of humour or delicacy of tact, often led him into absurd positions and incongruous statements which many a less talented man would have easily avoided; while his inordinate self-esteem, which at first stimulated him to a career of disinterested activity, degenerated in the latter part of his life into mere vanity and selfishness. He has been called "cold blooded"; this defect, however, existed more in appearance than in reality, for under the calm exterior of his phlegmatic and unimpassioned manner there undoubtedly lay a large amount of real sensibility and tenderness, and his writings show him to have been one of the most humanely minded men of the age in which he lived. Those who wish to estimate Godwin's character impartially will not judge him solely or chiefly, as hostile critics have done, by the odious traits which manifested themselves in his declining years, but will remember him also as he appeared in his early and better period, as the fearless champion of intellectual and social liberty, the author

of *Political Justice* and *Caleb Williams*, the husband
of Mary Wollstonecraft, and the sympathetic friend
and adviser of the many young enthusiasts who came
to him for assistance and encouragement.

A moralist who deals as frankly as Godwin did with
subjects which excite so much controversy, must necessarily be viewed in very different lights by those
who approve and those who reprobate his ideals.
"In weighing well his merits with his moral imperfections," says a writer of the latter class,[1] "it is melancholy to discover how far the latter preponderated,
and we are led to the very painful though certain conclusion, that it might have been better for mankind
had he never existed." This conclusion does not
strike every one now-a-days as possessing the certainty
attributed to it; nor has time altogether verified the
comfortable assertion, frequently advanced during the
past three-quarters of a century by those in whom the
wish was perhaps father to the thought, that Godwin's revolutionary theories have long been dead and
buried; for theories of this sort have a troublesome
habit of re-arising from the tomb at the very time
when their obsequies are being confidently celebrated.
A significant instance of this phenomenon may be
seen in Prof. W. Smyth's essay on Godwin,[2] in which,

---

[1] *Gentleman's Magazine*, obituary notice, June, 1836.
[2] *Lectures on the French Revolution*, vol. iii.

after stating that it is now impossible to read his works, as "the world is now in a more settled state, and people no longer make inquiries concerning political justice," he proceeds to explain that "this sentence was written many years ago, but I have lived to see all the doctrines of Godwin revived—they are the same as those which now infest the world and disgrace the human understanding, delivered by Mr. Owen, the Chartists, and the St. Simonians." This was written in 1842, and now, half a century later, the same might be said, *mutatis mutandis*, by the upholders of orthodoxy and constitutionalism.

Modern revolutionists, on the other hand, however little they may agree with portions of Godwin's work or approve his *a priori* method of reasoning, will feel that in choosing *Justice* for the watchword of his creed, in insisting on the liberty of individual opinion as distinct from the license of individual money-making, and in pointing with such emphasis to the accumulation of private property as the main cause of human wretchedness and depravity, he instinctively struck a true note, and entitled himself to be regarded as one of the pioneers of the great movement of social emancipation. A man of commanding genius he certainly was not; but it is equally certain that his abilities have in many quarters been unduly depreciated. There was more in Godwin, said Coleridge, than he was once willing to admit, though not so much as his enthusiastic admirers fancied; and this is perhaps the true and final judgment to be passed on him. One high quality, invaluable to a moralist, he undoubtedly possessed—the power of indoctrinating his readers with the intellectual enthusiasm by which he was himself inspired. "It was in the spring of this year," wrote one of Godwin's contemporaries in 1795,[1] "that I read a book which gave a turn to my mind, and directed the whole course of my life—a book which, after producing a powerful effect on the youth of that generation, has now sunk into unmerited oblivion. This was Godwin's *Political Justice.* In one respect the book had an excellent effect on my mind—it made me feel more *generously.* I had never felt before, nor, I am afraid, have I ever since felt so strongly, the duty of not living to one's self, but of having for one's sole object the good of the community."

It would be difficult to express more correctly the sum and substance of the teaching conveyed in Godwin's *Political Justice.*

H. S. SALT.

---

[1] Henry Crabb Robinson's *Diary*, i. 18.

LIST OF GODWIN'S CHIEF WORKS.

History of the Life of William Pitt, Lord Chatham,
8vo, 1783.

Sketches of History, in Six Sermons, 12mo, 1784.

An Enquiry concerning Political Justice, 2 vols., 4to,
1793.

Ditto, Second Edition, 2 vols., 8vo, 1796; Third
Edition, 1798. (A reprint was issued by James Wat-
son, the secularist, about 1840.)

*Things as they are, or the Adventures of Caleb
Williams,* a novel, 1794.

*The Enquirer; Reflections on Education, Manners,
and Literature,* 8vo, 1797.

Memoirs of Mary Wollstonecraft, 8vo, 1798.

St. Leon, a Tale of the Sixteenth Century, 4 vols.,
12mo, 1799.

Antonio, or the Soldier's Return, a Tragedy, 8vo,
1800.

A Reply to Dr. Parr and others, 8vo, 1801.

Life of Geoffrey Chaucer, 2 vols., 4to, 1803.

Fables, Ancient and Modern, 1805. (This was one of a series of educational works, written by Godwin under the pseudonym of Edward Baldwin.)

Fleetwood, or the New Man of Feeling, 3 vols., 12mo, 1805.

Faulkner, a tragedy, 1807.

Essay on Sepulchres, 16mo, 1809.

Lives of Edward and John Phillips, nephews of Milton, 4to, 1815.

Mandeville, a Tale of the Times of Cromwell, 3 vols., 8vo, 1817.

Of Population, an Answer to Malthus' Essay, 8vo, 1820.

A History of the Commonwealth of England, 4 vols., 1824–1828.

Cloudesly, a Tale, 12mo, 1830.

Thoughts on Man, a volume of Essays, 8vo, 1831.

Deloraine, a Novel, 3 vols., 1833.

Lives of the Necromancers, 8vo, 1834.

Essays, never before published, 1873.

AN ENQUIRY CONCERNING POLITICAL JUSTICE.

BOOK VIII.
OF PROPERTY.

CHAPTER I.

GENUINE SYSTEM OF PROPERTY DELINEATED.

IMPORTANCE OF THIS TOPIC.—ABUSES TO WHICH IT HAS
BEEN EXPOSED.—CRITERION OF PROPERTY : JUSTICE.—
ENTITLES EACH MAN TO THE SUPPLY OF HIS ANIMAL
WANTS AS FAR AS THE GENERAL STOCK WILL AFFORD
IT.—TO THE MEANS OF WELL BEING.—ESTIMATE OF
LUXURY.—ITS PERNICIOUS EFFECTS ON THE INDIVI-
DUAL WHO PARTAKES OF IT.—IDEA OF LABOUR AS THE
FOUNDATION OF PROPERTY CONSIDERED.—ITS UNREA-
SONABLENESS.—SYSTEM OF POPULAR MORALITY ON
THIS SUBJECT.—DEFECTS OF THAT SYSTEM.

THE subject of property is the key-stone that completes the fabric of political justice. According

as our ideas respecting it are crude or correct, they
will enlighten us as to the consequences of a *simple
form of society without government,* and remove the
prejudices that attach us to complexity.   There is
nothing that more powerfully tends to distort our
judgment and *opinions,* than erroneous notions concerning the goods of fortune. Finally, the period that
shall put an end to the system of *coercion* and *punishment,* is intimately connected with the circumstance of
property's being placed upon an equitable basis.

Various abuses of the most incontrovertible nature
have insinuated themselves into the administration of
property.   Each of these abuses might usefully be
made the subject of a separate investigation.   We
might inquire into the vexations of this sort that are
produced by the dreams of national greatness or magis-
tratical vanity.   This would lead us to a just estimate
of the different kinds of taxation, landed or mercantile, having the necessaries or the luxuries of life for
their subject of operation.   We might examine into
the abuses which have adhered to the commercial
system : monopolies, charters, patents, protecting
duties, prohibitions and bounties.   We might remark
upon the consequences that flow from the feudal
system and the system of ranks ; seignorial duties,
fines, conveyances, entails, estates freehold, copyhold
and manorial, vassalage and primogeniture.   We
might consider the rights of the church ; first fruits

and tithes : and we might enquire into the propriety
of the regulation by which a man, after having
possessed as sovereign a considerable property during
his life, is permitted to dispose of it at his pleasure,
at the period which the laws of nature seem to have
fixed as the termination of his authority. All these
enquiries would tend to show the incalculable importance of this subject. But, excluding them all from
the present enquiry, it shall be the business of what
remains of this work to consider, not any particular
abuses which have incidentally risen out of the administration of property, but those general principles
by which it has in almost all cases been directed, and
which, if erroneous, must not only be regarded as the
source of the abuses above enumerated, but of others
of innumerable kinds, too multifarious and subtle to
enter into so brief a catalogue.

What is the criterion that must determine whether
this or that substance, capable of contributing to the
benefit of a human being, ought to be considered as
your property or mine ? To this question there can
be but one answer—Justice. Let us then recur to
the principles of justice.[1]

---

[1] Book II., chap. ii. " Justice is a rule of conduct originat-
ing in the connection of one percipient being with another.
A comprehensive maxim which has been laid down upon
this subject is " that we should love our neighbours as ourselves." But this maxim, though possessing considerable

To whom does any article of property, suppose a loaf of bread, justly belong? To him who most wants it, or to whom the possession of it will be most beneficial. Here are six men famished with hunger, and the loaf is, absolutely considered, capable of satisfying the cravings of them all. Who is it that has a reasonable claim to benefit by the qualities with which this loaf is endowed? They are all brothers perhaps, and the law of primogeniture bestows it exclusively on the eldest. But does justice confirm this award? The laws of different countries dispose of property in a thousand different ways; but there can be but one way which is most comfortable to reason.

It would have been easy to put a case much stronger than that which has just been stated. I have an hundred loaves in my possession, and in the next street there is a poor man expiring with hunger, to whom one of these loaves would be the means of preserving his life. If I withhold this loaf from him, am I not unjust? If I impart it, am I not complying with what justice demands? To whom does the loaf justly belong?

I suppose myself in other respects to be in easy

---

merit as a popular principle, is not modelled with the strictness of philosophical accuracy." Godwin proceeds to argue that each person should be valued according to his usefulness to society, without regard to domestic ties and affections.

circumstances, and that I do not want this bread as an object of barter or sale, to procure me any of the other necessaries of a human being. Our animal wants have long since been defined, and are stated to consist of food, clothing and shelter. If justice have any meaning, nothing can be more iniquitous, than for one man to possess superfluities, while there is a human being in existence that is not adequately supplied with these.

Justice does not stop here. Every man is entitled, so far as the general stock will suffice, not only to the means of being, but of well being. It is unjust, if one man labour to the destruction of his health or his life, that another man may abound in luxuries. It is unjust, if one man be deprived of leisure to cultivate his rational powers, while another man contributes not a single effort to add to the common stock. The faculties of one man are like the faculties of another man. Justice directs that each man, unless perhaps he be employed more beneficially to the public, should contribute to the cultivation of the common harvest, of which each man consumes a share. This reciprocity indeed, as was observed when that subject was the matter of separate consideration, is of the very essence of justice. How the latter branch of it, the necessary labour, is to be secured, while each man is admitted to claim his share of the produce, we shall presently have occasion to enquire.

This subject will be placed in a still more striking light, if we reflect for a moment on the nature of luxuries. The wealth of any state may intelligibly enough be considered as the aggregate of all the incomes, which are annually consumed within that state, without destroying the materials of an equal consumption in the ensuing year. Considering this income as being, what in almost all cases it will be found to be, the produce of the industry of the inhabitants, it will follow that in civilized countries the peasant often does not consume more than the twentieth part of the produce of his labour, while his rich neighbour consumes perhaps the produce of the labour of twenty peasants. The benefit that arises to this favoured mortal ought surely to be very extraordinary.

But nothing is more evident than that the condition of this man is the reverse of beneficial. The man of an hundred pounds *per annum,* if he understand his own happiness, is a thousand times more favourably circumstanced. What shall the rich man do with his enormous wealth? Shall he eat of innumerable dishes of the most expensive viands, or pour down hogsheads of the most highly flavoured wines? A frugal diet will contribute infinitely more to health, to a clear understanding, to cheerful spirits, and even to the gratification of the appetites. Almost every other expense is an expense of ostentation. No man, but the most sordid epicure, would long continue to maintain even a plentiful table, if he had no spectators, visitors or servants, to behold his establishment. For whom are our sumptuous palaces and costly furniture, our equipages, and even our very clothes? The noble-man, who should for the first time let his imagination loose to conceive the style in which he would live, if he had nobody to observe, and no eye to please but his own, would no doubt be surprised to find that vanity had been the first mover in all his actions.

The object of this vanity is to procure the admira-tion and applause of beholders. We need not here enter into the intrinsic value of applause. Taking it for granted that it is as estimable an acquisition as any man can suppose it, how contemptible is the source of applause to which the rich man has re-course? "Applaud me, because my ancestor has left me a great estate." What merit is there in that? The first effect then of riches is to deprive their possessor of the genuine powers of understanding, and render him incapable of discerning absolute truth. They lead him to fix his affections on objects not accommodated to the wants and the structure of the human mind, and of consequence entail upon him disappointment and unhappiness. The greatest of all personal advantages are, independence of mind, which makes us feel that our satisfactions are not at the mercy either of men or of fortune; and activity of mind, the cheerfulness that arises from industry perpetually employed about objects, of which our judgment acknowledges the intrinsic value.

In this case we have compared the happiness of the man of extreme opulence with that of the man of one hundred pounds *per annum*. But the latter side of this alternative was assumed merely in compliance with existing prejudices. Even in the present state of human society we perceive, that a man, who should be perpetually earning the necessary competence by a very moderate industry, and with his pursuits uncrossed by the peevishness or caprice of his neighbours, would not be less happy than if he were born to that competence. In the state of society we are here contemplating, where, as will presently appear, the requisite industry will be of the lightest kind, it will be the reverse of a misfortune to any man, to find himself necessarily stimulated to a gentle activity, and in consequence to feel that no reverse of fortune could deprive him of the means of subsistence and contentment.

But it has been alleged, "that we find among different men very different degrees of labour and industry, and that it is not just they should receive an equal reward." It cannot indeed be denied that the attainments of men in virtue and usefulness ought by no means to be confounded. How far the present system of property contributes to their being equitably treated it is very easy to determine. The pre-

sent system of property confers on one man immense
wealth in consideration of the accident of his birth.
He that from beggary ascends to opulence is usually
known not to have effected this transition by methods
very creditable to his honesty or his usefulness. The
most industrious and active member of society is frequently with great difficulty able to keep his family
from starving.

But, to pass over these iniquitous effects of the
unequal distribution of property, let us consider the
nature of the reward which is thus proposed to industry. If you be industrious, you shall have an
hundred times more food than you can eat, and an
hundred times more clothes than you can wear. Where
is the justice of this? If I be the greatest benefactor
the human species ever knew, is that a reason for
bestowing on me what I do not want, especially when
there are thousands to whom my superfluity would be
of the greatest advantage? With this superfluity I
can purchase nothing but gaudy ostentation and envy,
nothing but the pitiful pleasure of returning to the
poor under the name of generosity that to which
reason gives them an irresistible claim, nothing but
prejudice, error and vice.

The doctrine of the injustice of accumulated property
has been the foundation of all religious morality. The
object of this morality has been, to excite men by
individual virtue to repair this injustice. The most

energetic teachers of religion have been irresistibly led to assert the precise truth upon this interesting subject. They have taught the rich, that they hold their wealth only as a trust, that they are strictly accountable for every atom of their expenditure, that they are merely administrators, and by no means proprietors in chief.[1] The defect of this system is, that they rather excite us to palliate our injustice than to forsake it.

No truth can be more simple than that which they inculcate. There is no action of any human being, and certainly no action that respects the disposition of property, that is not capable of better and worse, and concerning which reason and morality do not prescribe a specific conduct. He that sets out with acknowledging that other men are of the same nature as himself, and is capable of perceiving the precise place he would hold in the eye of an impartial spectator, must be fully sensible, that the money he employs in procuring an object of trifling or no advantage to himself, and which might have been employed in purchasing substantial and indispensable benefit to another, is unjustly employed. He that looks at his property with the eye of truth, will find that every shilling of it has received its destination from the dic-

---

[1] See *Swift's Sermon on Mutual Subjection*, quoted Book II. chap. ii. [Godwin's Note.]

tates of justice. He will at the same time, however, be exposed to considerable pain, in consequence of his own ignorance as to the precise disposition that justice and public utility require.

Does any man doubt of the truth of these assertions? Does any man doubt that, when I employ a sum of money small or great in the purchase of an absolute luxury for myself, I am guilty of vice? It is high time that this subject should be adequately understood. It is high time that we should lay aside the very names of justice and virtue, or that we should acknowledge that they do not authorise us to accumulate luxuries upon ourselves, while we see others in want of the indispensable means of improvement and happiness.

But, while religion inculcated on mankind the impartial nature of justice, its teachers have been too apt to treat the practice of justice, not as a debt, which it ought to be considered, but as an affair of spontaneous generosity and bounty. They have called upon the rich to be clement and merciful to the poor. The consequence of this has been that the rich, when they bestowed the most slender pittance of their enormous wealth in acts of charity, as they were called, took merit to themselves for what they gave, instead of considering themselves as delinquents for what they withheld.

Religion is in reality in all its parts an accommodation to the prejudices and weaknesses of mankind. Its authors communicated to the world as much truth as they calculated that the world would be willing to receive. But it is time that we should lay aside the instruction intended only for children in understanding,[1] and contemplate the nature and principles of things. If religion had spoken out, and told us it was just that all men should receive the supply of their wants, we should presently have been led to suspect that a gratuitous distribution to be made by the rich was a very indirect and ineffectual way of arriving at this object. The experience of all ages has taught us, that this system is productive only of a very precarious supply. The principal object which it seems to propose, is to place this supply in the disposal of a few, enabling them to make a show of generosity with what is not truly their own, and to purchase the gratitude of the poor by the payment of a debt. It is a system of clemency and charity, instead of a system of justice. It fills the rich with unreasonable pride by the spurious denominations with which it decorates their acts, and the poor with servility, by leading them to regard the slender comforts they obtain, not as their incontrovertible due, but as the good pleasure and the grace of their opulent neighbours.

---

[1] 1 Cor. iii. 1, 2. [Godwin's note.]

CHAPTER II.

BENEFITS ARISING FROM THE GENUINE SYSTEM OF PROPERTY.

CONTRASTED WITH THE MISCHIEFS OF THE PRESENT SYS-
TEM, AS CONSISTING—1. IN A SENSE OF DEPENDENCE.
2. IN THE PERPETUAL SPECTACLE OF INJUSTICE, LEAD-
ING MEN ASTRAY IN THEIR DESIRES—AND PERVERTING
THE INTEGRITY OF THEIR JUDGMENTS.—THE RICH ARE
THE TRUE PENSIONERS.—3. IN THE DISCOURAGEMENT
OF INTELLECTUAL ATTAINMENTS.—4. IN THE MULTI-
PLICATION OF VICE—GENERATING THE CRIMES OF THE
POOR—THE PASSIONS OF THE RICH—AND THE MISFOR-
TUNES OF WAR.—5. IN DEPOPULATION.

HAVING seen the justice of an equal distribution of property, let us next consider the benefits with which it would be attended. And here with grief it must be confessed, that, however great and extensive are the evils that are produced by monarchies and courts, by the imposture of priests and the iniquity of criminal laws, all these are imbecil and impotent compared with the evils that arise out of the established system of property.

Its first effect is that which we have already mentioned, a sense of dependence. It is true that courts are mean spirited, intriguing and servile, and that this disposition is transferred by contagion from them to all ranks of society. But property brings home a servile and truckling spirit by no circuitous method to every house in the nation. Observe the pauper fawning with abject vileness upon his rich benefactor, and speechless with sensations of gratitude for having received that which he ought to have claimed with an erect mien, and with a consciousness that his claim was irresistible. Observe the servants that follow in a rich man's train, watchful of his looks, anticipating his commands, not daring to reply to his insolence, all their time and their. efforts under the direction of his caprice. Observe the tradesman, how he studies the passions of his customers, not to correct, but to pamper them, the vileness of his flattery and the systematical constancy with which he exaggerates the merit of his commodities. Observe the practices of a popular election, where the great mass are purchased by obsequiousness, by intemperance and bribery, or driven by unmanly threats of poverty and persecution. Indeed " the age of chivalry is " not " gone ! "[1]

---

[1] *Burke's Reflections.*   [Godwin's note.]

The feudal spirit still survives, that reduced the great mass of mankind to the rank of slaves and cattle for the service of a few.

We have heard much of visionary and theoretical improvements. It would indeed be visionary and theoretical to expect virtue from mankind, while they are thus subjected to hourly corruption, and bred from father to son to sell their independence and their conscience for the vile rewards that oppression has to bestow. No man can be either useful to others or happy to himself who is a stranger to the grace of firmness, and who is not habituated to prefer the dictates of his own sense of rectitude to all the tyranny of command, and allurements of temptation. Here again, as upon a former occasion, religion comes in to illustrate our thesis. Religion was the generous ebullition of men, who let their imagination loose on the grandest subjects, and wandered without restraint in the unbounded field of inquiry. It is not to be wondered at therefore if they brought home imperfect ideas of the sublimest views that intellect can furnish. In this instance religion teaches that the true perfection of man is to divest himself of the influence of passions; that he must have no artificial wants, no sensuality, and no fear. But to divest the human species under the present system of the influence of passions is an extravagant speculation. The enquirer after truth and the benefactor of mankind

E

will be desirous of removing from them those external impressions by which their evil propensities are cherished. The true object that should be kept in view, is to extirpate all ideas of condescension and superiority, to oblige every man to feel, that the kindness he exerts is what he is bound to perform, and the assistance he asks what he has a right to claim.

A second evil that arises out of the established system of property is the perpetual spectacle of injustice it exhibits. This consists partly in luxury and partly in caprice. There is nothing more pernicious to the human mind than luxury. Mind, being in its own nature essentially active, necessarily fixes on some object public or personal, and in the latter case on the attainment of some excellence, or something which shall command the esteem and deference of others. No propensity, absolutely considered, can be more valuable than this. But the established system of property directs it into the channel of the acquisition of wealth. The ostentation of the rich perpetually goads the spectator to the desire of opulence. Wealth, by the sentiments of servility and dependence it produces, makes the rich man stand forward as the only object of general esteem and deference. In vain are sobriety, integrity, and industry, in vain the sublimest powers of mind and the most ardent benevolence, if their possessor be narrowed in his circumstances. To acquire wealth and to display it, is therefore the universal passion. The whole structure of human society is made a system of the narrowest selfishness. If self-love and benevolence were apparently reconciled as to their object, a man might set out with the desire of eminence, and yet every day become more generous and philanthropical in his views. But the passion we are here describing is accustomed to be gratified at every step by inhumanly trampling upon the interest of others. Wealth is acquired by overreaching our neighbours, and is spent in insulting them.

The spectacle of injustice which the established system of property exhibits, consists partly in caprice. If you would cherish in any man the love of rectitude, you must take care that its principles be impressed on him, not only by words, but actions. It sometimes happens during the period of education, that maxims of integrity and consistency are repeatedly enforced, and that the preceptor gives no quarter to the base suggestions of selfishness and cunning. But how is the lesson that has been read to the pupil confounded and reversed, when he enters upon the scene of the world? If he ask, " Why is this man honoured ? " the ready answer is, " Because he is rich." If he enquire further, " Why is he rich ? " the answer in most cases is, " From the accident of birth, or from a minute and sordid attention to the cares of gain."

The system of accumulated property is the offspring
of civil policy; and civil policy, as we are taught to
believe, is the production of accumulated wisdom.
Thus the wisdom of legislators and senates has been
employed, to secure a distribution of property the
most profligate and unprincipled, that bids defiance
to the maxims of justice and the nature of man.
Humanity weeps over the distresses of the peasantry
of all civilized nations; and, when she turns from
this spectacle to behold the luxury of their lords,
gross, imperious, and prodigal, her sensations certainly
are not less acute. This spectacle is the school in
which mankind have been educated. They have been
accustomed to the sight of injustice, oppression, and
iniquity, till their feelings are made callous, and their
understandings incapable of apprehending the nature
of true virtue.

In beginning to point out the evils of accumulated
property, we compared the extent of those evils with
the correspondent evils of monarchies and courts.
No circumstances under the latter have excited a
more pointed disapprobation than pensions and pecuniary corruption, by means of which hundreds of
individuals are rewarded, not for serving, but betray-
ing the public, and the hard earnings of industry are
employed to fatten the servile adherents of despotism. But the rent-roll of the lands of England is a
much more formidable pension list than that which

is supposed to be employed in the purchase of ministerial majorities. All riches, and especially all hereditary riches, are to be considered as the salary of a sinecure office, where the labourer and the manufacturer perform the duties, and the principal spends the income in luxury and idleness.[1] Hereditary

---

[1] This idea is to be found in Ogilvie's Essay on the Right of Property in Land, published about two years ago, Part I., Sect. iii. par. 38, 39. The reasonings of this author have sometimes considerable merit, though he has by no means gone to the source of the evil.

It might be amusing to some readers to recollect the authorities, if the citation of authorities were a proper mode of reasoning, by which the system of accumulated property is openly attacked. The best known is Plato, in his treatise of a Republic. His steps have been followed by Sir Thomas More, in his Utopia. Specimens of very powerful reasoning on the same side may be found in Gulliver's Travels, particularly, Part IV., chap. vi. Mably, in his book *De la Législation*, has displayed at large the advantages of equality, and then quits the subject in despair from an opinion of the incorrigibleness of human depravity. Wallace, the contemporary and antagonist of Hume, in a treatise entitled, Various Prospects of Mankind, Nature, and Providence, is copious in his eulogium of the same system, and deserts it only from fear of the earth becoming too populous: see below, Chap. VII. The great practical authorities are Crete, Sparta, Peru, and Paraguay. It would be easy to swell this list, if we added examples where an approach only to these principles was attempted, and authors who have incidentally confirmed a doctrine, so interesting and clear as never to have been wholly eradicated from any human understanding.

It would be trifling, to object that the systems of Plato and

wealth is in reality a premium paid to idleness, an immense annuity expended to retain mankind in brutality and ignorance. The poor are kept in ignorance by the want of leisure. The rich are furnished indeed with the means of cultivation and literature, but they are paid for being dissipated and indolent. The most powerful means that malignity could have invented, are employed to prevent them from improving their talents, and becoming useful to the public.

This leads us to observe, thirdly, that the established system of property is the true levelling system with respect to the human species, by as much as the cultivation of intellect and truth is more valuable and more characteristic of man, than the gratifications of vanity or appetite. Accumulated property treads the powers of thought in the dust, extinguishes the

---

others are full of imperfections. This indeed rather strengthens their authority; since the evidence of the truth they maintained was so great as still to preserve its hold on their understandings, though they knew not how to remove the difficulties that attended it. [Godwin's Note.]

William Ogilvie, referred to in this note, was an Aberdeen Professor, whose essay on the Land Question attracted some attention in 1781. It is strange that Godwin makes no mention of Thomas Spence, the forerunner of Henry George, whose lecture on Land Reform, read before the Newcastle Philosophical Society in 1775, had resulted in his expulsion from that body.

sparks of genius, and reduces the great mass of mankind to be immersed in sordid cares; beside depriving the rich, as we have already said, of the most salubrious and effectual motives to activity. If superfluity were banished, the necessity for the greater part of the manual industry of mankind would be superseded; and the rest, being amicably shared among all the active and vigorous members of the community, would be burdensome to none. Every man would have a frugal, yet wholesome diet; every man would go forth to that moderate exercise of his corporal functions that would give hilarity to the spirits; none would be made torpid with fatigue, but all would have leisure to cultivate the kindly and philanthropical affections of the soul, and to let loose his faculties in the search of intellectual improvement. What a contrast does this scene present us with the present state of human society, where the peasant and the labourer work till their understandings are benumbed with toil, their sinews contracted and made callous by being for ever on the stretch, and their bodies invaded with infirmities and surrendered to an untimely grave? What is the fruit of this disproportioned and unceasing toil? At evening they return to a family, famished with hunger, exposed half naked to the inclemencies of the sky, hardly sheltered, and denied the slenderest instruction, unless in a few instances, where it is dispensed by the hands of ostentatious charity, and the first lesson communicated is unprincipled servility. All this while their rich neighbour—but we visited him before.

How rapid and sublime would be the advances of intellect, if all men were admitted into the field of knowledge! At present ninety-nine persons in an hundred are no more excited to any regular exertions of general and curious thought, than the brutes themselves. What would be the state of public mind in a nation, where all were wise, all had laid aside the shackles of prejudice and implicit faith, all adopted with fearless confidence the suggestions of truth, and the lethargy of the soul was dismissed for ever? It is to be presumed that the inequality of mind would in a certain degree be permanent; but it is reasonable to believe that the geniuses of such an age would far surpass the grandest exertions of intellect that are at present known. Genius would not be depressed with false wants and niggardly patronage. It would not exert itself with a sense of neglect and oppression rankling in its bosom. It would be freed from those apprehensions that perpetually recall us to the thought of personal emolument, and of consequence would expatiate freely among sentiments of generosity and public good.

From ideas of intellectual let us turn to moral improvement. And here it is obvious that all the occasions of crime would be cut off for ever. All men love justice. All men are conscious that man is a being of one common nature, and feel the propriety of the treatment they receive from one another being measured by a common standard. Every man is desirous of assisting another; whether we should choose to ascribe this to an instinct implanted in his nature which renders this conduct a source of personal gratification, or to his perception of the reasonableness of such assistance. So necessary a part is this of the constitution of mind, that no man perpetrates any action, however criminal, without having first invented some sophistry, some palliation, by which he proves to himself that it is best to be done.[1] Hence it appears, that offence, the invasion of one man upon the security of another, is a thought alien to mind, and which nothing could have reconciled to us but the sharp sting of necessity. To consider merely the present order of human society, it is evident that the first offence must have been his who began a monopoly, and took advantage of the weakness of his neighbours to secure certain exclusive

---

[1] Book II., chap. iii. "The human mind is incredibly subtle in inventing an apology for that to which its inclination leads. Nothing is so rare as pure and unmingled hypocrisy. There is no action of our lives which we were not ready at the time of adopting it to justify, unless so far as we were prevented by mere indolence and unconcern."

privileges to himself. The man, on the other hand, who determined to put an end to this monopoly, and who peremptorily demanded what was superfluous to the possessor 'and would be of extreme benefit to himself, appeared to his own mind to be merely avenging the violated laws of justice. Were it not for the plausibleness of this apology, it is to be presumed that there would be no such thing as crime in the world.

The fruitful source of crimes consists in this circumstance, one man's possessing in abundance that of which another man is destitute. We must change the nature of mind, before we can prevent it from being powerfully influenced by this circumstance, when brought strongly home to its perceptions by the nature of its situation. Man must cease to have senses, the pleasures of appetite and vanity must cease to gratify, before he can look on tamely at the monopoly of these pleasures. He must cease to have a sense of justice, before he can clearly and fully approve this mixed scene of superfluity and distress. It is true that the proper method of curing this inequality is by reason and not by violence. But the immediate tendency of the established system is to persuade men that reason is impotent. The injustice of which they complain is upheld by force, and they are too easily induced by force to attempt its correction. All they endeavour is the partial correction of an injustice, which education tells them is necessary, but more powerful reason affirms to be tyrannical.

Force grew out of monopoly. It might accidentally have occurred among savages whose appetites exceeded their supply, or whose passions were inflamed by the presence of the object of their desire; but it would gradually have died away, as reason and civilization advanced. Accumulated property has fixed its empire; and henceforth all is an open contention of the strength and cunning of one party against the strength and cunning of the other. In this case the violent and premature struggles of the necessitous are undoubtedly an evil. They tend to defeat the very cause in the success of which they are most deeply interested; they tend to procrastinate the triumph of truth. But the true crime is in the malevolent and partial propensities of men, thinking only of themselves, and despising the emolument of others; and of these the rich have their share.

The spirit of oppression, the spirit of servility, and the spirit of fraud, these are the immediate growth of the established system of property. These are alike hostile to intellectual and moral improvement. The other vices of envy, malice, and revenge are their inseparable companions. In a state of society where men lived in the midst of plenty, and where all shared alike the bounties of nature, these sentiments would inevitably expire. The narrow principle of

selfishness would vanish. No man being obliged to
guard his little store, or provide with anxiety and
pain for his restless wants, each would lose his own
individual existence in the thought of the general
good. No man would be an enemy to his neighbour,
for they would have nothing for which to contend;
and of consequence philanthropy would resume the
empire which reason assigns her. Mind would be
delivered from her perpetual anxiety about corporal
support, and free to expatiate in the field of thought
which is congenial to her. Each man would assist
the enquiries of all.

Let us fix our attention for a moment upon the
revolution of principles and habits that immediately
grow out of an unequal distribution of property. Till
it was thus distributed, men felt what their wants
required, and sought the supply of those wants. All
that was more than this, was regarded as indifferent.
But no sooner is accumulation introduced, than they
begin to study a variety of methods for disposing of
their superfluity with least emolument to their neighbour, or in other words by which it shall appear to
be most their own. They do not long continue to
buy commodities, before they begin to buy men. He
that possesses or is the spectator of superfluity soon
discovers the hold which it affords us on the minds
of others. Hence the passions of vanity and ostentation. Hence the despotic manners of them who

recollect with complacence the rank they occupy, and the restless ambition of those whose attention is engrossed by the possible future.

Ambition is of all the passions of the human mind the most extensive in its ravages. It adds district to district, and kingdom to kingdom. It spreads bloodshed and calamity and conquest over the face of the earth. But the passion itself, as well as the means of gratifying it, is the produce of the prevailing system of property.[1] It is only by means of accumulation that one man obtains an unresisted sway over multitudes of others. It is by means of a certain distribution of income that the present governments of the world are retained in existence. Nothing more easy than to plunge nations so organized into war. But, if Europe were at present covered with inhabitants, all of them possessing competence, and none of them superfluity, what could induce its different countries to engage in hostility? If you would lead men to war, you must exhibit certain allurements. If you be not enabled by a system, already prevailing, and which derives force from prescription, to hire them to your purposes, you must bring over each individual by dint of persuasion. How hopeless a task by such

---

[1] Book V., chap. xvi. "A people among whom equality reigned, would possess everything they wanted, where they possessed the means of subsistence. Why should they pursue additional wealth or territory?"

means to excite mankind to murder each other! It is clear then that war in every horrid form is the growth of unequal property. As long as this source of jealousy and corruption shall remain, it is visionary to talk of universal peace. As soon as the source shall be dried up, it will be impossible to exclude the consequence. It is property that forms men into one common mass, and makes them fit to be played upon like a brute machine. Were this stumbling block removed, each man would be united to his neighbour in love and mutual kindness a thousand times more than now: but each man would think and judge for himself. Let then the advocates for the prevailing system, at least consider what it is for which they plead, and be well assured that they have arguments in its favour which will weigh against these disadvantages.

There is one other circumstance which, though inferior to those above enumerated, deserves to be mentioned. This is population. It has been calculated that the average cultivation of Europe might be improved, so as to maintain five times her present number of inhabitants.[1] There is a principle in human society by which population is perpetually kept down to the level of the means of subsistence. Thus among the wandering tribes of America and Asia, we never

---

[1] *Ogilvie*, Part i., Sect. iii., par. 35. [Godwin's note.]

find through the lapse of ages, that population has so increased, as to render necessary the cultivation of the earth. Thus, among the civilized nations of Europe, by means of territorial monopoly the sources of subsistence are kept within a certain limit, and, if the population became overstocked, the lower ranks of the inhabitants would be still more incapable of procuring for themselves the necessaries of life. There are no doubt extraordinary concurrences of circumstances, by means of which changes are occasionally introduced in this respect; but in ordinary cases the standard of population is held in a manner stationary for centuries. Thus the established system of property may be considered as strangling a considerable portion of our children in their cradle. Whatever may be the value of the life of man, or rather whatever would be his capability of happiness in a free and equal state of society, the system we are here opposing may be considered as arresting upon the threshold of existence four-fifths of that value and that happiness.

CHAPTER III.

OF THE OBJECTION TO THIS SYSTEM FROM THE ADMIRABLE EFFECTS OF LUXURY.

NATURE OF THE OBJECTION.—LUXURY NOT NECESSARY— EITHER TO POPULATION—OR TO THE IMPROVEMENT OF THE MIND.—ITS TRUE CHARACTER.

THESE ideas of justice and improvement are as old as literature and reflection themselves. They have suggested themselves in detached parts to the inquisitive in all ages, though they have perhaps never been brought together so as sufficiently to strike the mind with their consistency and beauty. But, after having furnished an agreeable dream, they have perpetually been laid aside as impracticable. We will proceed to examine the objections upon which this supposed impracticability has been founded; and the answer to these objections will gradually lead us to such a development of the proposed system, as by its completeness and the regular adjustment of its parts will be calculated to carry conviction to the most prejudiced mind.

64

There is one objection that has chiefly been cultivated on English ground, and to which we will give
the priority of examination. It has been affirmed
"that private vices are public benefits." But this
principle, thus coarsely stated by one of its original
advocates,[1] was remodelled by his more elegant suc-
cessors.[2] They observed, "that the true measure of
virtue and vice was utility, and consequently that it
was an unreasonable calumny to state luxury as a
vice. Luxury," they said, "whatever might be the
prejudices that cynics and ascetics had excited against
it, was the rich and generous soil that brought to
perfection the true prosperity of mankind. Without
luxury men must always have remained solitary
savages. It is luxury by which palaces are built and
cities peopled. How could there have been high
population in any country, without the various arts
in which the swarms of its inhabitants are busied?
The true benefactor of mankind is not the scrupulous
devotee who by his charities encourages insensibility
and sloth; is not the surly philosopher who reads
them lectures of barren morality; but the elegant
voluptuary who employs thousands in sober and
healthful industry to procure dainties for his table,
who unites distant nations in commerce to supply him

---

[1] Mandeville; *Fable of the Bees.* [Godwin's note.]
[2] Coventry, in a treatise entitled, *Philemon to Hydaspes:*
Hume; *Essays*, Part II, Essay II. [Godwin's note.]

F

with furniture, and who encourages the fine arts and all the sublimities of invention to furnish decorations for his residence."

I have brought forward this objection, rather that nothing material might appear to be omitted, than because it requires a separate answer. The true answer has been anticipated. It has been seen that the population of any country is measured by its cultivation. If therefore sufficient motives can be furnished to excite men to agriculture, there is no doubt, that population may be carried on to any extent that the land can be made to maintain. But agriculture, when once begun, is never found to stop in its career, but from positive discountenance. It is territorial monopoly that obliges men unwillingly to see vast tracts of land lying waste, or negligently and imperfectly cultivated, while they are subjected to the miseries of want. If land were perpetually open to him who was willing to cultivate it, it is not to be believed but that it would be cultivated in proportion to the wants of the community, nor by the same reason would there be any effectual check to the increase of population.

Undoubtedly the quantity of manual labour would be greatly inferior to that which is now performed by the inhabitants of any civilized country, since at present perhaps one-twentieth part of the inhabitants performs the agriculture which supports the whole.

But it is by no means to be admitted that this leisure would be found a real calamity.

As to what sort of a benefactor the voluptuary is to mankind, this was sufficiently seen when we treated of the effects of dependence and injustice. To this species of benefit all the crimes and moral evils of mankind are indebted for their perpetuity. If mind be to be preferred to mere animal existence, if it ought to be the wish of every reasonable enquirer, not merely that man, but that happiness should be propagated, then is the voluptuary the bane of the human species.

CHAPTER IV.

OF THE OBJECTION TO THIS SYSTEM FROM THE ALLUREMENTS OF SLOTH.

THE OBJECTION STATED.—SUCH A STATE OF SOCIETY MUST HAVE BEEN PRECEDED BY GREAT INTELLECTUAL IMPROVEMENT.—THE MANUAL LABOUR REQUIRED IN THIS STATE WILL BE EXTREMELY SMALL.—UNIVERSALITY OF THE LOVE OF DISTINCTION.—OPERATION OF THIS MOTIVE UNDER THE SYSTEM IN QUESTION.—WILL FINALLY BE SUPERSEDED BY A BETTER MOTIVE.

ANOTHER objection which has been urged against the system which counteracts the accumulation of property, is, "that it would put an end to industry. We behold in commercial countries the miracles that are operated by the love of gain. Their inhabitants cover the sea with their fleets, astonish mankind by the refinement of their ingenuity, hold vast continents in subjection in distant parts of the world by their arms, are able to defy the most powerful confederacies, and, oppressed with taxes and debts, seem to acquire fresh prosperity under their accumulated burthens. Shall we lightly part with a system that seems pregnant with such inexhaustible motives? Shall we believe that men will cultivate assiduously what they have no assurance they shall be permitted to apply to their personal emolument? It will perhaps be found with agriculture as it is with commerce, which then flourishes best when subjected to no control, but, when placed under rigid restraints, languishes and expires. Once establish it as a principle in society that no man is to apply to his personal use more than his necessities require, and you will find every man become indifferent to those exertions which now call forth the energy of his faculties. Man is the creature of sensations; and, when we endeavour to strain his intellect, and govern him by reason alone, we do but show our ignorance of his nature. Self-love is the genuine source of our actions,[1] and, if this should be found to bring vice and partiality along with it, yet the system that should endeavour to supersede it, would be at best no more than a beautiful romance. If each man found that, without being

---

[1] For an examination of this principle see Book IV., chap. viii. [Godwin's note.] Godwin here contends against the theory that virtue originates in self-interest. Man is "a being capable of justice, virtue, and benevolence, and who needs not always to be led to a philanthropical conduct by foreign and frivolous considerations."

compelled to exert his own industry, he might lay claim to the superfluity of his neighbour, indolence would perpetually usurp his faculties, and such a society must either starve, or be obliged in its own defence to return to that system of injustice and sordid interest, which theoretical reasoners will for ever arraign to no purpose."

This is the principal objection that prevents men from yielding without resistance to the accumulated evidence that has already been adduced. In reply, it may be observed in the first place, that the equality for which we are pleading is an equality that would succeed to a state of great intellectual improvement. So bold a revolution cannot take place in human affairs, till the general mind has been highly cultivated. The present age of mankind is greatly enlightened; but it is to be feared is not yet enlightened enough. Hasty and undigested tumults may take place under the idea of an equalization of property; but it is only a calm and clear conviction of justice, of justice mutually to be rendered and received, of happiness to be produced by the desertion of our most rooted habits, that can introduce an invariable system of this sort. Attempts without this preparation will be productive only of confusion. Their effect will be momentary, and a new and more barbarous inequality will succeed. Each man with unaltered appetite will watch his opportunity to gratify his love of power or his love of distinction, by usurping on his inattentive neighbours.

Is it to be believed then that a state of so great intellectual improvement can be the forerunner of barbarism? Savages, it is true, are subject to the weakness of indolence. But civilized and refined States are the scene of peculiar activity. It is thought, acuteness of disquisition, and ardour of pursuit, that set the corporeal faculties at work. Thought begets thought. Nothing can put a stop to the progressive advances of mind, but oppression. But here, so far from being oppressed, every man is equal, every man independent and at his ease. It has been observed that the establishment of a republic is always attended with public enthusiasm and irresistible enterprise. Is it to be believed that equality, the true republicanism, will be less effectual? It is true that in republics this spirit sooner or later is found to languish. Republicanism is not a remedy that strikes at the root of the evil. Injustice, oppression, and misery can find an abode in those seeming happy seats. But what shall stop the progress of ardour and improvement, where the monopoly of property is unknown?

This argument will be strengthened, if we reflect on the amount of labour that a state of equal property will require. What is this quantity of exertion from which we are supposing many members of the community to shrink? It is so light a burden as rather to assume the appearance of agreeable relaxation and gentle exercise, than of labour. In this community scarcely any can be expected in consequence of their situation or avocations to consider themselves as exempted from manual industry. There will be no rich men to recline in indolence and fatten upon the labour of their fellows. The mathematician, the poet, and the philosopher will derive a new stock of cheerfulness and energy from the recurring labour that makes them feel they are men. There will be no persons employed in the manufacture of trinkets and luxuries; and none in directing the wheels of the complicated machine of government, tax-gatherers, beadles, excisemen, tide-waiters, clerks, and secretaries. There will be neither fleets nor armies, neither courtiers nor footmen. It is the unnecessary employments that at present occupy the great mass of the inhabitants of every civilized nation, while the peasant labours incessantly to maintain them in a state more pernicious than idleness.

It has been computed that not more than one-twentieth of the inhabitants of England are employed seriously and substantially in the labours of agriculture. Add to this, that the nature of agriculture is such as necessarily to give full occupation in some parts of the year, and to leave others comparatively unemployed. We may consider these latter periods as equivalent to a labour which, under the direction of sufficient skill, might suffice in a simple state of society for the fabrication of tools, for weaving, and the occupation of tailors, bakers, and butchers. The object in the present state of society is to multiply labour, in another state it will be to simplify it. A vast disproportion of the wealth of the community has been thrown into the hands of a few, and ingenuity has been continually upon the stretch to find out ways in which it may be expended. In the feudal times the great lord invited the poor to come and eat of the produce of his estate upon condition of their wearing his livery, and forming themselves in rank and file to do honour to his well-born guests. Now that exchanges are more facilitated, we have quitted this inartificial mode, and oblige the men we maintain out of our incomes to exert their ingenuity and industry in return. Thus, in the instance just mentioned, we pay the tailor to cut our clothes to pieces, that he may sew them together again, and to decorate them with stitching and various ornaments, without which experience would speedily show that they were in no respect less useful. We are imagining in the present case a state of the most rigid simplicity.

From the sketch which has been here given it seems by no means impossible that the labour of every twentieth man in the community would be sufficient to maintain the rest in all the absolute necessaries of human life. If then this labour, instead of being performed by so small a number, were amicably divided

among them all, it would occupy the twentieth part
of every man's time. Let us compute that the industry of a labouring man engrosses ten hours in every
day, which, when we have deducted his hours of rest,
recreation, and meals, seems an ample allowance. It
follows that half an hour a day, seriously employed in
manual labour by every member of the community,
would sufficiently supply the whole with necessaries.
Who is there that would shrink from this degree of
industry ? Who is there that sees the incessant
industry exerted in this city and this island, and
would believe that with half an hour's industry *per
diem,* we should be every way happier and better
than we are at present ? Is it possible to contemplate
this fair and generous picture of independence and
virtue, where every man would have ample leisure for
the noblest energies of mind, without feeling our very
souls refreshed with admiration and hope ?

When we talk of men's sinking into idleness if they
be not excited by the stimulus of gain, we have certainly very little considered the motives that at present
govern the human mind. We are deceived by the
apparent mercenariness of mankind, and imagine that
the accumulation of wealth is their great object. But
the case is far otherwise. The present ruling passion
of the human mind is the love of distinction. There
is no doubt a class in society that are perpetually
urged by hunger and need, and have no leisure for

motives less gross and material. But is the class next above them less industrious than they? I exert a certain species of industry to supply my immediate wants; but these wants are soon supplied. The rest is exerted that I may wear a better coat, that I may clothe my wife in gay attire, that I may not merely have a shelter, but a handsome habitation, not merely bread or flesh to eat, but that I may set it out with a suitable decorum. How many of these things would engage my attention, if I lived in a desert island, and had no spectators of my economy? If I survey the appendages of my person, is there one article that is not an appeal to the respect of my neighbours, or a refuge against their contempt? It is for this that the merchant braves the dangers of the ocean, and the mechanical inventor brings forth the treasures of his meditation. The soldier advances even to the cannon's mouth, the statesman exposes himself to the rage of an indignant people, because they cannot bear to pass through life without distinction and esteem. Exclusively of certain higher motives that will presently be mentioned, this is the purpose of all the great exertions of mankind. The man who has nothing to provide for but his animal wants, scarcely ever shakes off the lethargy of his mind; but the love of praise hurries us on to the most incredible achievements. Nothing is more common than to find persons who surpass the rest of their species in activity, inexcusably remiss in the amelioration of their pecuniary affairs.

In reality, those by whom this reasoning has been urged have mistaken the nature of their own objection. They did not sincerely believe that men could be roused into action only by the love of gain; but they imagined that in a state of equal property men would have nothing to occupy their attention. What degree of truth there is in this idea we shall presently have occasion to estimate.

Meanwhile it is sufficiently obvious, that the motives which arise from the love of distinction are by no means cut off, by a state of society incompatible with the accumulation of property. Men, no longer able to acquire the esteem or avoid the contempt of their neighbours by circumstances of dress and furniture, will divert the passion for distinction into another channel. They will avoid the reproach of indolence, as carefully as they now avoid the reproach of poverty. The only persons who at present neglect the effect which their appearance and manners may produce, are those whose faces are ground with famine and distress. But in a state of equal society no man will be oppressed, and of consequence the more delicate affections of the soul will have time to expand themselves. The general mind having, as we have already shown, arrived at a high pitch of improvement, the impulse that carries it out into action will be stronger than ever. The fervour of public spirit will be great. Leisure will be multiplied, and the leisure of a cultivated understanding is the precise period in which great designs, designs the tendency of which is to secure applause and esteem, are conceived. In tranquil leisure it is impossible for any but the sublimest mind to exist without the passion for distinction. This passion, no longer permitted to lose itself in indirect channels and useless wanderings, will seek the noblest course, and perpetually fructify the seeds of public good. Mind, though it will perhaps at no time arrive at the termination of its possible discoveries and improvements, will nevertheless advance with a rapidity and firmness of progression of which we are at present unable to conceive the idea.

The love of fame is no doubt a delusion. This like every other delusion will take its turn to be detected and abjured. It is an airy phantom, which will indeed afford us an imperfect pleasure so long as we worship it, but will always in a considerable degree disappoint us, and will not stand the test of examination. We ought to love nothing but good, a pure and immutable felicity, the good of the majority, the good of the general. If there be anything more substantial than all the rest, it is justice, a principle that rests upon this single postulatum, that man and man are beings of the same nature, and susceptible, under certain limitations, of the same advantages. Whether the benefit proceed from you or me, so it be but conferred, is a pitiful distinction. / Justice has the further advantage, which serves us as a countercheck to prove the goodness of this species of arithmetic, of producing the only solid happiness to the man by whom it is practised, as well as the good of all. But fame cannot benefit me, any more than serve the best purposes to others. The man who acts from the love of it, may produce public good; but, if he do, it is from indirect and spurious views. Fame is an unsubstantial and delusive pursuit. If it signify an opinion entertained of me greater than I deserve, to pursue it is vicious. If it be the precise mirror of my character, it is desirable only as a means, inasmuch as I may perhaps be able to do most good to the persons who best know the extent of my capacity and the rectitude of my intentions.

The love of fame, when it perishes in minds formed under the present system, often gives place to a greater degeneracy. Selfishness is the habit that grows out of monopoly. When therefore this selfishness ceases to seek its gratification in public exertion, it too often narrows itself into some frigid conception of personal pleasure, perhaps sensual, perhaps intellectual. But this cannot be the process where monopoly is banished. Selfishness has there no kindly circumstances to foster it. Truth, the overpowering truth of general good, then seizes us irresistibly. It is impossible we should want motives, so long as we see clearly how multitudes and ages may be benefited by our exertions, how causes and effects are connected in an endless chain, so that no honest effort can be lost, but will operate to good, centuries after its author is consigned to the grave. This will be the general passion, and all will be animated by the example of all.

CHAPTER V.

OF THE OBJECTION TO THIS SYSTEM FROM THE IMPOSSIBILITY OF ITS BEING RENDERED PERMANENT.

GROUNDS OF THE OBJECTION.—ITS SERIOUS IMPORT.— ANSWER.—THE INTRODUCTION OF SUCH A SYSTEM MUST BE OWING, 1. TO A DEEP SENSE OF JUSTICE.—2. TO A CLEAR INSIGHT INTO THE NATURE OF HAPPINESS —AS BEING PROPERLY INTELLECTUAL—NOT CONSIST- ING IN SENSUAL PLEASURE—OR THE PLEASURES OF DELUSION.—INFLUENCE OF THE PASSIONS CONSIDERED. —MEN WILL NOT ACCUMULATE EITHER FROM INDIVI- DUAL FORESIGHT—OR FROM VANITY.

LET us proceed to another objection. It has some- times been said by those who oppose the doc- trine here maintained, "that equality might perhaps contribute to the improvement and happiness of man- kind, if it were consistent with the nature of man that such a principle should be rendered permanent; but that every expectation of that kind must prove abor- tive. Confusion would be introduced under the idea of equality to-day, but the old vices and monopolies would return to-morrow. All that the rich would have purchased by the most generous sacrifice, would be a period of barbarism, from which the ideas and regulations of civil society must commence as from a new infancy. The nature of man cannot be changed. There would at least be some vicious and designing members of society, who would endeavour to secure to themselves indulgences beyond the rest. Mind would not be reduced to that exact uniformity which a state of equal property demands; and the variety of sentiments which must always in some degree prevail, would inevitably subvert the refined systems of speculative perfection."

No objection can be more essential than that which is here adduced. It highly becomes us in so momentous a subject to resist all extravagant speculations : it would be truly to be lamented, if, while we parted with that state of society through which mind has been thus far advanced, we were replunged into barbarism by the pursuit of specious appearances. But what is worst of all is, that, if this objection be true, it is to be feared there is no remedy. Mind must go forward. What it sees and admires, it will some time or other seek to attain. Such is the inevitable law of our nature. But it is impossible not to see the beauty of equality, and to be charmed with the benefits it seems to promise. The consequence is sure. Man,

G

according to the system of these reasoners, is prompted to advance for some time with success; but after that time, in the very act of pursuing further improvement, he necessarily plunges beyond the compass of his powers, and has then his petty career to begin afresh. The objection represents him as a foul abortion, with just understanding enough to see what is good, but with too little to retain him in the practice of it. Let us consider whether equality, once established, would be so precarious as it is here represented.

In answer to this objection it must first be remembered, that the state of equalization we are here supposing is not the result of accident, of the authority of a chief magistrate, or the over-earnest persuasion of a few enlightened thinkers, but is produced by the serious and deliberate conviction of the community at large. We will suppose for the present that it is possible for such a conviction to take place among a given number of persons living in society with each other: and, if it be possible in a small community, there seems to be no sufficient reason to prove that it is impossible in one of larger and larger dimensions. The question we have here to examine is concerning the probability, when the conviction has once been introduced, of its becoming permanent.

The conviction rests upon two intellectual impressions, one of justice, and the other of happiness.

Equalization of property cannot begin to assume a fixed appearance in human society, till the sentiment becomes deeply wrought into the mind, that the genuine wants of any man constitute his only just claim to the appropriating any species of commodity. If the general sense of mankind were once so far enlightened, as to produce a perpetual impression of this truth, of so forcible a sort as to be exempt from all objections and doubt, we should look with equal horror and contempt at the idea of any man's accumulating a property he did not want. All the evils that a state of monopoly never fails to engender would stand forward in our minds, together with all the existing happiness that attended upon a state of freedom. We should feel as much alienation of thought from the consuming uselessly upon ourselves what would be beneficial to another, or from the accumulating property for the purpose of obtaining some kind of ascendancy over the mind of our neighbours, as we now feel from the commission of murder. No man will dispute, that a state of equal property once established, would greatly diminish the evil propensities of man. But the crime we are now supposing is more atrocious than any that is to be found in the present state of society. Man perhaps is incapable under any circumstance of perpetrating an action of which he has a clear and undoubted perception that it is contrary to the general good. But be this as it will, it

is hardly to be believed that any man for the sake
of some imaginary gratification to himself would
wantonly injure the whole, if his mind were not first
ulcerated with the impression of the injury that
society by its ordinances is committing against him.
The case we are here considering is that of a man,
who does not even imagine himself injured, and yet
wilfully subverts a state of happiness to which no
description can do justice, to make room for the
return of all those calamities and vices with which
mankind have been infested from the earliest page of
history.

The equalization we are describing is further indebted for its empire in the mind to the ideas with
which it is attended of personal happiness. It grows
out of a simple, clear and unanswerable theory of the
human mind, that we first stand in need of a certain
animal subsistence and shelter, and after that, that our
only true felicity consists in the expansion of our
intellectual powers, the knowledge of truth, and the
practice of virtue. It might seem at first sight as if
this theory omitted a part of the experimental history
of the mind, the pleasures of sense, and the pleasures
of delusion. But this omission is apparent, not real.
However many are the kinds of pleasure of which we
are susceptible, the truly prudent man will sacrifice
the inferior to the more exquisite. Now no man who
has ever produced or contemplated the happiness of

others with a liberal mind, will deny that this exercise is infinitely the most pleasurable of all sensations. But he that is guilty of the smallest excess of sensual pleasures, by so much diminishes his capacity of obtaining this highest pleasure. Not to add, if that be of any importance, that rigid temperance is the reasonable means of tasting sensual pleasures with the highest relish. This was the system of Epicurus, and must be the system of every man who ever speculated deeply on the nature of human happiness. For the pleasures of delusion, they are absolutely incompatible with our highest pleasure. If we would either promote or enjoy the happiness of others, we must seek to know in what it consists. But knowledge is the irreconcilable foe of delusion. In proportion as mind rises to its true element, and shakes off those prejudices which are the authors of our misery, it becomes incapable of deriving pleasure from flattery, fame, or power, or indeed from any source that is not compatible with, or, in other words, does not make a part of the common good. The most palpable of all classes of knowledge is that I am, personally considered, but an atom in the ocean of mind.—The first rudiment, therefore, of that science of personal happiness which is inseparable from a state of equalization, is, that I shall derive infinitely more pleasure from simplicity, frugality, and truth, than from luxury, empire, and fame. What temptation has a man, entertaining this opinion, and living in a state of equal property, to accumulate ?

This question has been perpetually darkened by the doctrine, so familiar to writers of morality, of the independent operations of reason and passion. Such distinctions must always darken. Of how many parts does mind consist? Of none. It consists merely of a series of thought succeeding thought from the first moment of our existence to its termination. This word passion, which has produced such extensive mischief in the philosophy of mind, and has no real archetype, is perpetually shifting its meaning. Sometimes it is applied universally to all those thoughts, which, being peculiarly vivid, and attended with great force of argument real or imaginary, carry us out into action with uncommon energy. Thus we speak of the passion of benevolence, public spirit, or courage. Sometimes it signifies those vivid thoughts only which upon accurate examination appear to be founded in error. In the first sense the word might have been unexceptionable. Vehement desire is the result of a certain operation of the understanding, and must always be in a joint ratio of the supposed clearness of the proposition and importance of the practical effects. In the second sense, the doctrine of the passions would have been exceedingly harmless, if we had been accustomed to put the definition instead of the thing defined. It would then

have been found that it merely affirmed that the
human mind must always be liable to precisely the
same mistakes as we observe in it at present, or in
other words affirmed the necessary permanence in
opposition to the necessary perfectibility of intellect.
Who is there indeed that sees not, in the case above
stated, the absurdity of supposing a man, so long as
he has a clear view of justice and interest lying on
one side of a given question, to be subject to errors
that irresistibly compel him to the other? The mind
is no doubt liable to fluctuation. But there is a degree of conviction that would render it impossible for
us any longer to derive pleasure from intemperance,
dominion or fame, and this degree in the incessant
progress of thought must one day arrive.

This proposition of the permanence of a system of
equal property, after it has once been brought into
action by the energies of reason and conviction, will
be placed out of the reach of all equitable doubt, if
we proceed to form to ourselves an accurate picture
of the action of this system. Let us suppose that we
are introduced to a community of men, who are accustomed to an industry proportioned to the wants of
the whole, and to communicate instantly and uncon-
ditionally, each man to his neighbour, that for which
the former has not and the latter has immediate occasion. Here the first and simplest motive to personal
accumulation is instantly cut off. I need not accumu-

late to protect myself against accidents, sickness or
infirmity, for these are claims the validity of which is
not regarded as a subject of doubt, and with which
every man is accustomed to comply.   I can accumulate in a considerable degree nothing but what is
perishable, for exchange being unknown, that which
I cannot personally consume adds nothing to the sum
of my wealth.—Meanwhile it should be observed that,
though accumulation for private purposes under such
a system would be in the highest degree irrational
and absurd, this by no means precludes such accumulation as may be necessary to provide against public
contingencies.   If there be any truth in the preceding
reasonings, this kind of accumulation will be unat-
tended with danger.   Add to this, that the perpetual
tendency of wisdom is to preclude contingency.   It is
well known that dearths are principally owing to the
false precautions and false timidity of mankind; and
it is reasonable to suppose that a degree of skill will
hereafter be produced which will gradually annihilate
the failure of crops and other similar accidents.

It has already appeared that the principal and
unintermitting motive to private accumulation is the
love of distinction and esteem.   This motive is also
withdrawn.   As accumulation can have no rational
object, it would be viewed as a mark of insanity, not
a title to admiration.   Men would be accustomed to
the simple principles of justice, and know that nothing

was entitled to esteem but talents and virtue. Habituated to employ their superfluity to supply the wants of their neighbour, and to dedicate the time which was not necessary for manual labour to the cultivation of intellect, with what sentiments would they behold the man who was foolish enough to sew a bit of lace upon his coat, or affix any other ornament to his person? In such a community property would perpetually tend to find its level. It would be interesting to all to be informed of the person in whose hands a certain quantity of any commodity was lodged, and every man would apply with confidence to him for the supply of his wants in that commodity. Putting therefore out of the question every kind of compulsion, the feeling of depravity and absurdity that would be excited with relation to the man who refused to part with that for which he had no real need would operate in all cases as a sufficient discouragement to so odious an innovation. Every man would conceive that he had a just and complete title to make use of my superfluity. If I refused to listen to reason and expostulation on this head, he would not stay to adjust with me a thing so vicious as exchange, but would leave me in order to seek the supply from some rational being. Accumulation, instead, as now, of calling forth every mark of respect, would tend to cut off he individual who attempted it from all the bonds of society, and sink him in neglect and oblivion.

The influence of accumulation at present is derived from the idea of eventual benefit in the mind of the observer; but the accumulator then would be in a case still worse than that of the miser now, who, while he adds thousands to his heap, cannot be prevailed upon to part with a superfluous farthing, and is therefore the object of general desertion.

CHAPTER VI.

OF THE OBJECTION TO THIS SYSTEM FROM THE INFLEXIBILITY OF ITS RESTRICTIONS.

NATURE OF THE OBJECTION.—NATURAL AND MORAL INDE-
PENDENCE DISTINGUISHED—THE FIRST BENEFICIAL—
THE SECOND INJURIOUS.—TENDENCY OF RESTRICTION
PROPERLY SO CALLED.—THE GENUINE SYSTEM OF PRO-
PERTY NOT A SYSTEM OF RESTRICTIONS—DOES NOT
REQUIRE COMMON LABOUR, MEALS OR MAGAZINES.—
SUCH RESTRICTIONS ABSURD—AND UNNECESSARY.—
EVILS OF CO-OPERATION.—ITS PROVINCE MAY PER-
PETUALLY BE DIMINISHED.—MANUAL LABOUR MAY BE
EXTINGUISHED.—CONSEQUENT ACTIVITY OF INTELLECT.
IDEAS OF THE FUTURE STATE OF CO-OPERATION.—ITS
LIMITS.—ITS LEGITIMATE PROVINCE.—EVILS OF CO-
HABITATION—AND MARRIAGE.—THEY OPPOSE THE
DEVELOPMENT OF OUR FACULTIES—ARE INIMICAL TO
OUR HAPPINESS—AND DEPRAVE OUR UNDERSTANDINGS.
—MARRIAGE A BRANCH OF THE PREVAILING SYSTEM
OF PROPERTY.—CONSEQUENCES OF ITS ABOLITION.—
EDUCATION NEED NOT IN THAT STATE OF SOCIETY BE

A SUBJECT OF POSITIVE INSTITUTION.—THESE PRIN-
CIPLES DO NOT LEAD TO A SULLEN INDIVIDUALITY.—
PARTIAL ATTACHMENTS CONSIDERED.—BENEFITS AC-
CRUING FROM A JUST AFFECTION—MATERIALLY PRO-
MOTED BY THESE PRINCIPLES.—THE GENUINE SYSTEM
OF PROPERTY DOES NOT PROHIBIT ACCUMULATION—
IMPLIES A CERTAIN DEGREE OF APPROPRIATION—AND
DIVISION OF LABOUR.

AN objection that has often been urged against a
system of equal property is, "that it is inconsistent with personal independence. Every man according to this scheme is a passive instrument in the
hands of the community. He must eat and drink
and play and sleep at the bidding of others. He has
no habitation, no period at which he can retreat into
himself, and not ask another's leave. He has nothing
that he can call his own, not even his time or his
person. Under the appearance of a perfect freedom
from oppression and tyranny, he is in reality subjected
to the most unlimited slavery."

To understand the force of this objection it is
necessary that we should distinguish two sorts of independence, one of which may be denominated natural
and the other moral. Natural independence, a freedom from all constraint except that of reason and
argument presented to the understanding, is of the
utmost importance to the welfare and improvement of

mind. Moral independence on the contrary is always injurious. The dependence which is essential in this respect to the wholesome temperament of society, includes in it articles that are no doubt unpalatable to a multitude of the present race of mankind, but that owe their unpopularity only to weakness and vice. It includes a censure to be exercised by every individual over the actions of another, a promptness to inquire into them, and to judge them. Why should I shrink from this? What could be more beneficial than for each man to derive every possible assistance for correcting and moulding his conduct from the perspicacity of his neighbours? The reason why this species of censure is at present exercised with illiberality, is because it is exercised clandestinely, and we submit to its operation with impatience and aversion. Moral independence is always injurious: for, as has abundantly appeared in the course of the present inquiry, there is no situation in which I can be placed where it is not incumbent upon me to adopt a certain species of conduct in preference to all others, and of consequence where I shall not prove an ill member of society if I act in any other than a particular manner. The attachment that is felt by the present race of mankind to independence in this respect, the desire to act as they please without beng accountable to the principles of reason, is highly detrimental to the general welfare.

But, if we ought never to act independently of the principles of reason, and in no instance to shrink from the candid examination of another, it is nevertheless essential that we should at all times be free to cultivate the individuality and follow the dictates of our own judgment. If there be anything in the scheme of equal property that infringes this principle, the objection is conclusive. If the scheme be, as it has often been represented, a scheme of government, constraint and regulation, it is no doubt in direct hostility with the principles of this work.

But the truth is, that a system of equal property requires no restrictions or superintendence whatever. There is no need of common labour, common meals or common magazines. These are feeble and mistaken instruments for restraining the conduct without making conquest of the judgment. If you cannot bring over the hearts of the community to your party, expect no success from brute regulations. If you can, regulation is unnecessary. Such a system was well enough adapted to the military constitution of Sparta; but it is wholly unworthy of men who are enlisted in no cause but that of reason and justice. Beware of reducing men to the state of machines. Govern them through no medium but that of inclination and conviction.

Why should we have common meals? Am I obliged to be hungry at the same time that you are? Ought

I to come at a certain hour, from the museum where I am working, the recess where I meditate, or the observatory where I remark the phenomena of nature, to a certain hall appropriated to the office of eating; instead of eating, as reason bids me, at the time and place most suited to my avocations? Why have common magazines? For the purpose of carrying our provisions a certain distance, that we may afterwards bring them back again? Or is this precaution really necessary, after all that has been said in praise of equal society and the omnipotence of reason, to guard us against the knavery and covetousness of our associates? If it be, for God's sake let us discard the parade of political justice, and go over to the standard of those reasoners who say, that man and the practice of justice are incompatible with each other.

Once more let us be upon our guard against reducing men to the condition of brute machines. The objectors of the last chapter were partly in the right when they spoke of the endless variety of mind. It would be absurd to say that we are not capable of truth, of evidence and agreement. In these respects, so far as mind is in a state of progressive improvement, we are perpetually coming nearer to each other. But there are subjects about which we shall continually differ, and ought to differ. The ideas, the associations and the circumstances of each man are properly his own; and it is a pernicious system that would lead

us to require all men, however different their circumstances, to act in many of the common affairs of life
by a precise general rule. Add to this, that, by the
doctrine of progressive improvement, we shall always
be erroneous, though we shall every day become less
erroneous. The proper method for hastening the
decay of error, is not, by brute force, or by regulation
which is one of the classes of force, to endeavour to
reduce men to intellectual uniformity ; but on the
contrary by teaching every man to think for himself.

From these principles it appears that everything
that is usually understood by the term co-operation, is
in some degree an evil. A man in solitude is obliged
to sacrifice or postpone the execution of his best
thoughts to his own convenience. How many admirable designs have perished in the conception by means
of this circumstance! The true remedy is for men to
reduce their wants to the fewest possible, and as much
as possible to simplify the mode of supplying them.
It is still worse when a man is also obliged to consult
the convenience of others. If I be expected to eat or
to work in conjunction with my neighbour, it must
either be at a time most convenient to me, or to him,
or to neither of us. We cannot be reduced to a clock-
work uniformity.

Hence it follows that all supererogatory co-operation is carefully to be avoided, common labour and
common meals. "But what shall we say to co-opera-

tion that seems to be dictated by the nature of the work to be performed?" It ought to be diminished. At present it is unreasonable to doubt, that the consideration of the evil of co-operation is in certain urgent cases to be postponed to that urgency. Whether by the nature of things co-operation of some sort will always be necessary, is a question that we are scarcely competent to decide. At present, to pull down a tree, to cut a canal, to navigate a vessel, requires the labour of many. Will it always require the labour of many? When we look at the complicated machines of human contrivance, various sorts of mills, of weaving engines, of steam engines, are we not astonished at the compendium of labour they produce? Who shall say where this species of improvement must stop? At present such inventions alarm the labouring part of the community; and they may be productive of temporary distress, though they conduce in the sequel to the most important interests of the multitude. But in a state of equal labour their utility will be liable to no dispute. Hereafter it is by no means clear that the most extensive operations will not be within the reach of one man; or, to make use of a familiar instance, that a plough may not be turned into a field, and perform its office without the need of superintendence. It was in this sense that the celebrated Franklin conjectured, that " mind would one day become omnipotent over matter."

H

The conclusion of the progress which has here been sketched, is something like a final close to the necessity of manual labour. It is highly instructive in such cases to observe how the sublime geniuses of former times anticipated what seems likely to be the future improvement of mankind. It was one of the laws of Lycurgus, that no Spartan should be employed in manual labour. For this purpose under his system it was necessary that they should be plentifully supplied with slaves devoted to drudgery. Matter, or, to speak more accurately, the certain and unintermitting laws of the universe, will be the Helots of the period we are contemplating. We shall end in this respect, oh immortal legislator! at the point from which you began.

To these prospects perhaps the objection will once again be repeated, "that men, delivered from the necessity of manual labour, will sink into supineness." What narrow views of the nature and capacities of mind do such objections imply! The only thing necessary to put intellect into action is motive. Are there no motives equally cogent with the prospect of hunger? Whose thoughts are most active, most rapid and unwearied, those of Newton or the ploughman? When the mind is stored with prospects of intellectual greatness and utility, can it sink into torpor?

To return to the subject of co-operation. It may be

a curious speculation to attend to the progressive steps by which this feature of human society may be expected to decline. For example : shall we have concerts of music ? The miserable state of mechanism of the majority of the performers is so conspicuous, as to be even at this day a topic of mortification and ridicule. Will it not be practicable hereafter for one man to perform the whole ? Shall we have theatrical exhibitions ? This seems to include an absurd and vicious co-operation. It may be doubted whether men will hereafter come forward in any mode gravely to repeat words and ideas not their own. It may be doubted whether any musical performer will habitually execute the compositions of others. We yield supinely to the superior merit of our predecessors, because we are accustomed to indulge the inactivity of our own faculties. All formal repetition of other men's ideas seems to be a scheme for imprisoning for so long a time the operations of our own mind. It borders perhaps in this respect upon a breach of sincerity, which requires that we should give immediate utterance to every useful and valuable idea that occurs to our thoughts.

Having ventured to state these hints and conjectures, let us endeavour to mark the limits of individuality. Every man that receives an impression from any external object, has the current of his own thoughts modified by force; and yet without external impressions we should be nothing. We ought not, except under certain limitations, to endeavour to free ourselves from their approach. Every man that reads the composition of another, suffers the succession of his ideas to be in a considerable degree under the direction of his author. But it does not seem as if this would ever form a sufficient objection against reading. One man will always have stored up reflections and facts that another wants; and mature and digested discourse will perhaps always, in equal circumstances, be superior to that which is extempore. Conversation is a species of co-operation, one or the other party always yielding to have his ideas guided by the other : and yet conversation and the intercourse of mind with mind seem to be the most fertile sources of improvement. It is here as it is with punishment. He that in the gentlest manner undertakes to reason another out of his vices, will probably occasion pain; but this species of punishment ought upon no account to be superseded.

Another article which belongs to the subject of co-operation is cohabitation. A very simple process will lead us to a right decision in this instance. Science is most effectually cultivated, when the greatest number of minds are employed in the pursuit of it. If a hundred men spontaneously engage the whole energy of their faculties upon the solution of a given question, the chance of success will be greater

than if only ten men were so employed. By the same
reason the chance will be also increased, in proportion
as the intellectual operations of these men are individual, in proportion as their conclusions are directed
by the reason of the thing, uninfluenced by the force
either of compulsion or sympathy. All attachments to
individuals, except in proportion to their merits, are
plainly unjust. It is therefore desirable, that we
should be the friends of man rather than of particular
men, and that we should pursue the chain of our own
reflections, with no other interruption than informa-
tion or philanthropy requires.

This subject of cohabitation is particularly interesting, as it includes in it the subject of marriage. It
will therefore be proper to extend our inquiries somewhat further upon this head. Cohabitation is not only
an evil, as it checks the independent progress of mind,
it is also inconsistent with the imperfections and propensities of man. It is absurd to expect that the
inclinations and wishes of two human beings should
coincide through any long period of time. To oblige
them to act and to live together, is to subject them
to some inevitable portion of thwarting, bickering and
unhappiness. This cannot be otherwise, so long as
man has failed to reach the standard of absolute perfection. The supposition that I must have a companion for life, is the result of a complication of vices.
It is the dictate of cowardice, and not of fortitude. It

flows from the desire of being loved and esteemed for something that is not desert.

But the evil of marriage as it is practised in European countries lies deeper than this. The habit is, for a thoughtless and romantic youth of each sex to come together, to see each other for a few times and under circumstances full of delusion, and then to vow to each other eternal attachment. What is the consequence of this? In almost every instance they find themselves deceived. They are reduced to make the best of an irretrievable mistake. They are presented with the strongest imaginable temptation to become the dupes of falsehood. They are led to conceive it their wisest policy to shut their eyes upon realities, happy if by any perversion of intellect they can persuade themselves that they were right in their first crude opinion of their companion. The institution of marriage is a system of fraud; and men who carefully mislead their judgments in the daily affair of their life, must always have a crippled judgment in every other concern. We ought to dismiss our mistake as soon as it is detected; but we are taught to cherish it. We ought to be incessant in our search after virtue and worth; but we are taught to check our inquiry, and shut our eyes upon the most attractive and admirable objects. Marriage is law, and the worst of all laws. Whatever our understandings may tell us of the person from whose connection we should derive the greatest improvement, of the worth of one woman and the demerits of another, we are obliged to consider what is law, and not what is justice.

Add to this, that marriage is an affair of property, and the worst of all properties. So long as two human beings are forbidden by positive institution to follow the dictates of their own mind, prejudice is alive and vigorous. So long as I seek to engross one woman to myself, and to prohibit my neighbour from proving his superior desert and reaping the fruits of it, I am guilty of the most odious of all monopolies. Over this imaginary prize men watch with perpetual jealousy, and one man will find his desires and his capacity to circumvent as much excited, as the other is excited to traverse his projects and frustrate his hopes. As long as this state of society continues, philanthropy will be crossed and checked in a thousand ways, and the still augmenting stream of abuse will continue to flow.

The abolition of marriage will be attended with no evils. We are apt to represent it to ourselves as the harbinger of brutal lust and depravity. But it really happens in this as in other cases, that the positive laws which are made to restrain our vices, irritate and multiply them. Not to say, that the same sentiments of justice and happiness which in a state of equal property would destroy the relish for luxury, would decrease our inordinate appetites of every kind, and lead us universally to prefer the pleasures of intellect to the pleasures of sense.

The intercourse of the sexes will in such a state fall under the same system as any other species of friendship. Exclusively of all groundless and obstinate attachments, it will be impossible for me to live in the world without finding one man of a worth superior to that of any other whom I have an opportunity of observing. To this man I shall feel a kindness in exact proportion to my apprehension of his worth. The case will be precisely the same with respect to the female sex. I shall assiduously cultivate the intercourse of that woman whose accomplishments shall strike me in the most powerful manner. " But it may happen that other men will feel for her the same preference that I do." This will create no difficulty. We may all enjoy her conversation; and we shall all be wise enough to consider the sensual intercourse as a very trivial object. This, like every other affair in which two persons are concerned, must be regulated in each successive instance by the unforced consent of either party. It is a mark of the extreme depravity of our present habits, that we are inclined to suppose the sensual intercourse anywise material to the advantages arising from the purest affection. Reasonable men now eat and drink, not from the love of pleasure, but because eating and drinking are essential to our healthful existence. Reasonable men then will propagate their species, not because a certain sensible pleasure is annexed to this action, but because it is right the species should be propagated; and the manner in which they exercise this function will be regulated by the dictates of reason and duty.

Such are some of the considerations that will probably regulate the commerce of the sexes. It cannot be definitely affirmed whether it will be known in such a state of society who is the father of each individual child. But it may be affirmed that such knowledge will be of no importance. It is aristocracy, self-love and family pride that teach us to set a value upon it at present. I ought to prefer no human being to another, because that being is my father, my wife, or my son, but because, for reasons which equally appeal to all understandings, that being is entitled to preference. One among the measures which will successively be dictated by the spirit of democracy, and that probably at no great distance, is the abolition of surnames.

Let us consider the way in which this state of society will modify education. It may be imagined that the abolition of marriage would make it in a certain sense the affair of the public; though, if there be any truth in the reasonings of this work, to provide for it by the positive institutions of a community,

would be extremely inconsistent with the true prin-
ciples of the intellectual system.[1]   Education may be
regarded as consisting of various branches.   First,
the personal cares which the helpless state of an
infant requires.   These will probably devolve upon
the mother; unless, by frequent parturition or by the
very nature of these cares, that were found to render
her share of the burthen unequal; and then it would
be amicably and willingly participated by others.
Secondly, food and other necessary supplies.   These,
as we have already seen, would easily find their true
level, and spontaneously flow from the quarter in
which they abounded to the quarter that was deficient.
Lastly, the term education may be used to signify
instruction.   The task of instruction, under such a
form of society as that we are contemplating, will be
greatly simplified and altered from what it is at
present.   It will then be thought no more legitimate
to make boy slaves, than to make men so.   The
business will not then be to bring forward so many
adepts in the egg-shell, that the vanity of parents
may be flattered by hearing their praises.   No man
will then think of vexing with premature learning the
feeble and inexperienced, for fear that, when they

---

[1] In Book VI., chap. viii., Godwin contends against a
system of national education, on the ground that it stereo-
types and retards thought.

came to years of discretion, they should refuse to be learned. Mind will be suffered to expand itself in proportion as occasion and impression shall excite it, and not tortured and enervated by being cast in a particular mould. No creature in human form will be expected to learn anything, but because he desires it and has some conception of its utility and value; and every man, in proportion to his capacity, will be ready to furnish such general hints and comprehensive views, as will suffice for the guidance and encouragement of him who studies from a principle of desire.

Before we quit this part of the subject it will be necessary to obviate an objection that will suggest itself to some readers. They will say "that man was formed for society and reciprocal kindness; and therefore is by his nature little adapted to the system of individuality which is here delineated. The true perfection of man is to blend and unite his own existence with that of another, and therefore a system which forbids him all partialities and attachments, tends to degeneracy and not to improvement."

No doubt man is formed for society. But there is a way in which, for a man to lose his own existence in that of others, that is eminently vicious and detrimental. Every man ought to rest upon his own centre, and consult his own understanding. Every man ought to feel his independence, that he can assert the principles of justice and truth, without being obliged treacherously to adapt them to the peculiarities of his situation, and the errors of others.

No doubt man is formed for society. But he is formed for, or in other words his faculties enable him to serve, the whole and not a part. Justice obliges us to sympathise with a man of merit more fully than with an insignificant and corrupt member of society. But all partialities strictly so called, tend to the injury of him who feels them, of mankind in general, and even of him who is their object. The spirit of partiality is well expressed in the memorable saying of Themistocles, "God forbid that I should sit upon a bench of justice, where my friends found no more favour than strangers!" In fact, as has been repeatedly seen in the course of this work, we sit in every action of our lives upon a bench of justice; and play in humble imitation the part of the unjust judge, whenever we indulge the smallest atom of partiality.

Such are the limitations of the social principle. These limitations in reality tend to improve it and render its operations beneficial. It would be a miserable mistake to suppose that the principle is not of the utmost importance to mankind. All that in which the human mind differs from the intellectual principle in animals is the growth of society. All that is excellent in man is the fruit of progressive improvement, of the circumstance of one age taking advantage of the discoveries of a preceding age, and setting out from the point at which they had arrived.

Without society we should be wretchedly deficient in motives to improvement. But what is most of all, without society our improvements would be nearly useless. Mind without benevolence is a barren and a cold existence. It is in seeking the good of others, in embracing a great and expansive sphere of action, in forgetting our own individual interests, that we find our true element. The tendency of the whole system delineated in this Book is to lead us to that element. The individuality it recommends tends to the good of the whole, and is valuable only as a means to that end. Can that be termed a selfish system, where no man desires luxury, no man dares to be guilty of injustice, and every one devotes himself to supply the wants, animal or intellectual, of others ?— To proceed.

As a genuine state of society is incompatible with all laws and restrictions, so it cannot have even this restriction, that no man shall amass property. The security against accumulation, as has already been said, lies in the perceived absurdity and inutility of accumulation. The practice, if it can be conceived in a state of society where the principles of justice were adequately understood, would not even be dangerous. The idea would not create alarm, as it is apt to do in prospect among the present advocates of political justice. Men would feel nothing but their laughter or their pity excited at so strange a perversity of human intellect.

What would denominate anything my property? The fact, that it was necessary to my welfare. My right would be coeval with the existence of that necessity. The word property would probably remain; its signification only would be modified. The mistake does not so properly lie in the idea itself, as in the source from which it is traced. What I have, if it be necessary for my use, is truly mine; what I have, though the fruit of my own industry, if unnecessary, it is an usurpation for me to retain.

Force in such a state of society would be unknown; I should part with nothing without a full consent. Caprice would be unknown; no man would covet that which I used, unless he distinctly apprehended that it would be more beneficial in his possession than it was in mine. My apartment would be as sacred to a certain extent as it is at present. No man would obtrude himself upon me to interrupt the course of my studies and meditations. No man would feel the whim of occupying my apartment, while he could provide himself another as good of his own. That which was my apartment yesterday would probably be my apartment to-day. We have few pursuits that do not require a certain degree of apparatus; and it would be for the general good that I should find in ordinary cases the apparatus ready for my use to-day that I left yesterday. But, though the idea of property thus modified would remain, the jealousy and selfishness of property would be gone. Bolts and locks would be unknown. Every man would be welcome to make every use of my accommodations that did not interfere with my own use of them. Novices as we are, we may figure to ourselves a thousand disputes, where property was held by so slight a tenure. But disputes would in reality be impossible. They are the offspring of a misshapen and disproportioned love of ourselves. Do you want my table? Make one for yourself; or, if I be more skilful in that respect than you, I will make one for you. Do you want it immediately? Let us compare the urgency of your wants and mine, and let justice decide.

These observations lead us to the consideration of one additional difficulty, which relates to the division of labour. Shall each man make all his tools, his furniture and accommodations? This would perhaps be a tedious operation. Every man performs the task to which he is accustomed more skilfully and in a shorter time than another. It is reasonable that you should make for me, that which perhaps I should be three or four times as long making, and should make imperfectly at last. Shall we then introduce barter and exchange? By no means. The abstract spirit of exchange will perhaps govern; every man will

employ an equal portion of his time in manual labour.
But the individual application of exchange is of all
practices the most pernicious.   The moment I require
any other reason for supplying you than the cogency
of your claim, the moment, in addition to the dictates
of benevolence, I demand a prospect of advantage to
myself, there is an end of that political justice and
pure society of which we treat.   No man will have a
trade.   It cannot be supposed that a man will con-
struct any species of commodity, but in proportion as
it is wanted.   The profession paramount to all others,
and in which every man will bear his part, will be that
of man, and in addition perhaps that of cultivator.

The division of labour, as it has been treated by
commercial writers, is for the most part the offspring
of avarice.   It has been found that ten persons can
make two hundred and forty times as many pins in
a day as one person.[1]   This refinement is the growth
of luxury.   The object is to see into how vast a sur-
face the industry of the lower classes may be beaten,
the more completely to gild over the indolent and the
proud.   The ingenuity of the merchant is whetted by
new improvements of this sort to transport more of
the wealth of the powerful into his own coffers.   The
possibility of effecting a compendium of labour by

---

[1] Smith's *Wealth of Nations*, Book I., chap. i.   [Godwin's
note.

this means will be greatly diminished, when men shall learn to deny themselves superfluities. The utility of such a saving of labour, where labour is so little, will scarcely balance against the evils of so extensive a co-operation. From what has been said under this head, it appears that there will be a division of labour, if we compare the society in question with the state of the solitaire and the savage. But it will produce an extensive composition of labour, if we compare it with that to which we are at present accustomed in civilized Europe.

CHAPTER VII.

OF THE OBJECTION TO THIS SYSTEM FROM THE PRINCIPLE OF POPULATION.

THE OBJECTION STATED.—REMOTENESS OF ITS OPERATION.
—CONJECTURAL IDEAS RESPECTING THE ANTIDOTE.—
OMNIPOTENCE OF MIND.—ILLUSTRATIONS.—CAUSES OF
DECREPITUDE.—YOUTH IS PROLONGED BY CHEERFUL-
NESS—BY CLEARNESS OF APPREHENSION—AND A
BENEVOLENT CHARACTER.—THE POWERS WE POSSESS
ARE ESSENTIALLY PROGRESSIVE.—EFFECTS OF ATTEN-
TION.—THE PHENOMENON OF SLEEP EXPLAINED.—
PRESENT UTILITY OF THESE REASONINGS.—APPLICA-
TION TO THE FUTURE STATE OF SOCIETY.

AN author who has speculated widely upon subjects of government,[1] has recommended equal
or, which was rather his idea, common property, as a
complete remedy, to the usurpation and distress which

---

[1] Wallace: *Various Prospects of Mankind, Nature and
Providence*, 1761. [Godwin's Note.]

are at present the most powerful enemies of human kind, to the vices which infect education in some instances, and the neglect it encounters in more, to all the turbulence of passion, and all the injustice of selfishness. But, after having exhibited this picture, not less true than delightful, he finds an argument that demolishes the whole, and restores him to indifference and despair, in the excessive population that would ensue.

One of the most obvious answers to this objection is, that to reason thus is to foresee difficulties at a great distance. Three-fourths of the habitable globe is now uncultivated. The parts already cultivated are capable of immeasurable improvement. Myriads of centuries of still increasing population may probably pass away, and the earth still be found sufficient for the subsistence of its inhabitants. Who can say how long the earth itself will survive the casualties of the planetary system? Who can say what remedies shall suggest themselves for so distant an inconvenience, time enough for practical application, and of which we may yet at this time have not the smallest idea? It would be truly absurd for us to shrink from a scheme of essential benefit to mankind, lest they should be too happy, and by necessary consequence at some distant period too populous.

But, though these remarks may be deemed a sufficient answer to the objection, it may not be amiss to indulge in some speculations to which such an objection obviously leads. The earth may, to speak in the style of one of the writers of the Christian Scriptures, "abide for ever." [1] It may be in danger of becoming too populous. A remedy may then be necessary. If it may, why should we sit down in supine indifference and conclude that we can discover no glimpse of it? The discovery, if made, would add to the firmness and consistency of our prospects; nor is it improbable to conjecture that that which would form the regulating spring of our conduct then, might be the medium of a salutary modification now. What follows must be considered in some degree as a deviation into the land of conjecture. If it be false, it leaves the great system to which it is appended in all sound reason as impregnable as ever. If this do not lead us to the true remedy, it does not follow that there is no remedy. The great object of inquiry will still remain open, however defective may be the suggestions that are now to be offered.

Let us here return to the sublime conjecture of Franklin, that "mind will one day become omnipotent over matter." If over all other matter, why not over the matter of our own bodies? If over matter at ever so great a distance, why not over matter which, however ignorant we may be of the tie that connects

---

[1] Ecclesiastes i. 4. [Godwin's Note.]

it with the thinking principle, we always carry about with us, and which is in all cases the medium of communication between that principle and the external universe ? In a word, why may not man be one day immortal ?

The different cases in which thought modifies the external universe are obvious to all. It is modified by our voluntary thoughts or design. We desire to stretch out our hand, and it is stretched out. We perform a thousand operations of the same species every day, and their familiarity annihilates the wonder. They are not in themselves less wonderful than any of those modifications which we are least accustomed to conceive. Mind modifies body involuntarily. Emotion excited by some unexpected word, by a letter that is delivered to us, occasions the most extraordinary revolutions in our frame, accelerates the circulation, causes the heart to palpitate, the tongue to refuse its office, and has been known to occasion death by extreme anguish or extreme joy. These symptoms we may either encourage or check. By encouraging them habits are produced of fainting or of rage. To discourage them is one of the principal offices of fortitude. The effort of mind in resisting pain in the stories of Cranmer and Mucius Scævola is of the same kind. It is reasonable to believe that that effort with a different direction might have cured certain diseases of the system. There is nothing

indeed of which physicians themselves are more frequently aware, than of the power of the mind in
assisting or retarding convalescence.

Why is it that a mature man soon loses that
elasticity of limb which characterizes the heedless
gaiety of youth? Because he desists from youthful
habits. He assumes an air of dignity incompatible
with the lightness of childish sallies. He is visited
and vexed with all the cares that rise out of our
mistaken institutions, and his heart is no longer
satisfied and gay. Hence his limbs become stiff and
unwieldy. This is the forerunner of old age and
death.

The first habit favourable to corporeal vigour is
cheerfulness. Every time that our mind becomes
morbid, vacant and melancholy, a certain period is
cut off from the length of our lives. Listlessness of
thought is the brother of death. But cheerfulness
gives new life to our frame and circulation to our
juices. Nothing can long be stagnant in the frame
of him, whose heart is tranquil, and his imagination
active.

A second requisite in the case of which we treat is
a clear and distinct conception. If I know precisely
what I wish, it is easy for me to calm the throbs
of pain, and to assist the sluggish operations of the
system. It is not a knowledge of anatomy, but a
quiet and steady attention to my symptoms, that will

best enable me to correct the distemper from which they spring. Fainting is nothing else but a confusion of mind, in which the ideas appear to mix in painful disorder, and nothing is distinguished.

The true source of cheerfulness is benevolence. To a youthful mind, while everything strikes with its novelty, the individual situation must be peculiarly unfortunate, if gaiety of thought be not produced, or, when interrupted, do not speedily return with its healing oblivion. But novelty is a fading charm, and perpetually decreases. Hence the approach of inanity and listlessness. After we have made a certain round, life delights no more. A deathlike apathy invades us. Thus the aged are generally cold and indifferent; nothing interests their attention, or rouses the sluggishness of their soul. How should it be otherwise? The pursuits of mankind are commonly frigid and contemptible, and the mistake comes at last to be detected. But virtue is a charm that never fades. The soul that perpetually overflows with kindness and sympathy, will always be cheerful. The man who is perpetually busied in contemplations of public good, will always be active.

The application of these reasonings is simple and irresistible. If mind be now in a great degree the ruler of the system, why should it be incapable of extending its empire? If our involuntary thoughts can derange or restore the animal economy, why

should we not in process of time, in this as in other
instances, subject the thoughts which are at present
involuntary to the government of design ?   If volition
can now do something, why should it not go on to do
still more and more ?   There is no principle of reason
less liable to question than this, that, if we have in
any respect a little power now, and if mind be essentially progressive, that power may, and, barring any
extraordinary concussions of nature, infallibly will,
extend beyond any bounds we are able to prescribe
to it.

Nothing can be more irrational and presumptuous
than to conclude, because a certain species of supposed power is entirely out of the line of our present
observations, that it is therefore altogether beyond
the limits of the human mind.   We talk familiarly
indeed of the limits of our faculties, but nothing is
more difficult than to point them out.   Mind, in a
progressive view at least, is infinite.   If it could have
been told to the savage inhabitants of Europe in the
times of Theseus and Achilles, that man was capable
of predicting eclipses and weighing the air, of ex-
plaining the phenomena of nature so that no prodigies
should remain, of measuring the distance and the size
of the heavenly bodies, this would not have appeared
to them less wonderful, than if we had told them of
the possible discovery of the means of maintaining
the human body in perpetual youth and vigour.   But

we have not only this analogy, showing that the discovery in question forms as it were a regular branch of the acquisitions that belong to an intellectual nature; but in addition to this we seem to have a glimpse of the specific manner in which the acquisition will be secured. Let us remark a little more distinctly the simplicity of the process.

We have called the principle of immortality in man cheerfulness, clearness of conception, and benevolence. Perhaps we shall in some respects have a more accurate view of its potency, if we consider it as of the nature of attention. It is a very old maxim of practical conduct, that whatever is done with attention, is done well. It is because this was a principal requisite, that many persons endowed in an eminent degree with cheerfulness, perspicacity, and benevolence, have perhaps not been longer lived than their neighbours. We are not capable at present of attending to everything. A man who is engaged in the sublimest and most delightful exertions of mind, will perhaps be less attentive to his animal functions than his most ordinary neighbour, though he will frequently in a partial degree repair that neglect, by a more cheerful and animated observation, when those exertions are suspended. But, though the faculty of attention may at present have a very small share of ductility, it is probable that it may be improved in that respect to an inconceivable degree. The picture

that was exhibited of the subtlety of mind in an
earlier stage of this work,[1] gives to this supposition
a certain degree of moral evidence. If we can have
three hundred and twenty successive ideas in a second
of time, why should it be supposed that we shall not
hereafter arrive at the skill of carrying on a great
number of contemporaneous processes without disorder?

Having thus given a view of. what may be the
future improvement of mind, it is proper that we
should qualify this picture to the sanguine temper of
some readers and the incredulity of others, by observing that this improvement, if capable of being realized,
is however at a great distance. A very obvious
remark will render this eminently palpable. If an
unintermitted attention to the animal economy be
necessary, then, before death can be banished, we
must banish sleep, death's image. Sleep is one of the
most conspicuous infirmities of the human frame. It
is not, as has often been supposed, a suspension of
thought, but an irregular and distempered state of the
faculty. Our tired attention resigns the helm, ideas
swim before us in wild confusion, and are attended
with less and less distinctness, till at length they

---

[1] "We have a multitude of different successive perceptions
in every moment of our existence." Book IV., Chap. vii.,
p. 330.

leave no traces in the memory. Whatever attention and volition are then imposed upon us, as it were at unawares, are but faint resemblances of our operations in the same kind when awake. Generally speaking, we contemplate sights of horror with little pain, and commit the most atrocious crimes with little sense of their true nature. The horror we sometimes attribute to our dreams, will frequently be found upon accurate observation to belong to our review of them when we wake.

One other remark may be proper in this place. If the remedies here prescribed tend to a total extirpation of the infirmities of our nature, then, though we cannot promise to them an early and complete success, we may probably find them of some utility now. They may contribute to prolong our vigour, though not to immortalize it, and, which is of more consequence, to make us live while we live. Every time the mind is invaded with anguish and gloom, the frame becomes disordered. Every time that languor and indifference creep upon us, our functions fall into decay. In proportion as we cultivate fortitude and equanimity, our circulations will be cheerful. In proportion as we cultivate a kind and benevolent propensity, we may be secure of finding something for ever to interest and engage us.

Medicine may reasonably be stated to consist of two branches, the animal and intellectual. The latter

of these has been infinitely too much neglected. It
cannot be employed to the purposes of a profession ;
or, where it has been incidentally so employed, it has
been artificially and indirectly, not in an open and
avowed manner. "Herein the patient must minister
to himself." [1] How often do we find a sudden piece
of good news dissipating a distemper! How common
is the remark, that those accidents, which are to the
indolent a source of disease, are forgotten and extirpated in the busy and active! It would no doubt be
of extreme moment to us, to be thoroughly acquainted
with the power of motives, habit, and what is called
resolution, in this respect. I walk twenty miles in
an indolent and half-determined temper, and am extremely fatigued. I walk twenty miles full of ardour
and with a motive that engrosses my soul, and I come
in as fresh and alert as when I began my journey.
We are sick and we die, generally speaking, because
we consent to suffer these accidents. This consent
in the present state of mankind is in some degree
unavoidable. We must have stronger motives and
clearer views, before we can uniformly refuse it. But,
though we cannot always, we may frequently refuse.
This is a truth of which all mankind are to a certain
degree aware. Nothing more common than for the
most ignorant man to call upon his sick neighbour, to

---

[1] Macbeth, Act V. [Godwin's Note.]

rouse himself, not to suffer himself to be conquered; and this exhortation is always accompanied with some consciousness of the efficacy of resolution. The wise and the good man therefore should carry with him the recollection of what cheerfulness and a determined spirit are able to do, of the capacity with which he is endowed of expelling the seeds and first slight appearances of indisposition.

The principal part of the preceding paragraph is nothing more than a particular application of what was elsewhere delivered respecting moral and physical causes.[1] It would have been easy to have cast the present chapter in a different form, and to have made it a chapter upon health, showing that one of the advantages of a better state of society would be a very high improvement of the vigour and animal constitution of man. In that case the conjecture of immortality would only have come in as an incidental remark, and the whole would have assumed less the air of conjecture than of close and argumentative deduction. But it was perhaps better to give the

---

[1] Godwin's argument is that the mind is more powerful than the physical conditions of climate, etc. " Our communication with the material universe is at the mercy of our choice; and the inability of the understanding for intellectual exertion is principally an affair of moral consideration, existing only in the degree in which it is deliberately preferred." Book I., Chap. vii., Part I.

subject the most explicit form, at the risk of exciting
a certain degree of prejudice.

To apply these remarks to the subject of population. The tendency of a cultivated and virtuous mind
is to render us indifferent to the gratifications of
sense. They please at present by their novelty, that
is, because we know not how to estimate them. They
decay in the decline of life indirectly because the
system refuses them, but directly and principally
because they no longer excite the ardour and passion
of mind. It is well known that an inflamed imagination is capable of doubling and tripling the seminal
secretions. The gratifications of sense please at
present by their imposture. We soon learn to despise
the mere animal function, which, apart from the
delusions of intellect, would be nearly the same in all
cases; and to value it, only as it happens to be re-
lieved by personal charms or mental excellence. We
absurdly imagine that no better road can be found to
the sympathy and intercourse of minds. But a very
slight degree of attention might convince us that this
is a false road, full of danger and deception. Why
should I esteem another, or by another be esteemed?
For this reason only, because esteem is due, and only
so far as it is due.

The men therefore who exist when the earth shall
refuse itself to a more extended population, will cease
to propagate, for they will no longer have any motive,

either of error or duty, to induce them. In addition
to this they will perhaps be immortal. The whole
will be a people of men, and not of children. Generation will not succeed generation, nor truth have in a
certain degree to recommence her career at the end of
every thirty years. There will be no war, no crimes,
no administration of justice as it is called, and no
government. These latter articles are at no great
distance; and it is not impossible that some of the
present race of men may live to see them in part
accomplished. But beside this, there will be no disease, no anguish, no melancholy, and no resentment.
Every man will seek with ineffable ardour the good
of all. Mind will be active and eager, yet never
disappointed. Men will see the progressive advance-
ment of virtue and good, and feel that, if things
occasionally happen contrary to their hopes, the
miscarriage itself was a necessary part of that progress. They will know, that they are members of the
chain, that each has his several utility, and they will
not feel indifferent to that utility. They will be eager
to inquire into the good that already exists, the means
by which it was produced, and the greater good that
is yet in store. They will never want motives for
exertion; for that benefit which a man thoroughly
understands and earnestly loves, he cannot refrain
from endeavouring to promote.

Before we dismiss the subject it is proper once again

to remind the reader, that the leading doctrine of this chapter is given only as matter of probable conjecture, and that the grand argument of this division of the work is altogether independent of its truth or falsehood.

CHAPTER VIII.

OF THE MEANS OF INTRODUCING THE GENUINE SYSTEM OF PROPERTY.

APPREHENSIONS THAT ARE ENTERTAINED ON THIS SUBJECT. — IDEA OF MASSACRE. — INFERENCE WE OUGHT TO MAKE UPON SUPPOSITION OF THE REALITY OF THESE APPREHENSIONS.—MISCHIEF BY NO MEANS THE NECESSARY ATTENDANT ON IMPROVEMENT.—DUTIES UNDER THIS CIRCUMSTANCE, 1. OF THOSE WHO ARE QUALIFIED FOR PUBLIC INSTRUCTORS — TEMPER — SINCERITY.— PERNICIOUS EFFECTS OF DISSIMULATION IN THIS CASE. —2. OF THE RICH AND GREAT.—MANY OF THEM MAY BE EXPECTED TO BE ADVOCATES OF EQUALITY. —CONDUCT WHICH THEIR INTEREST AS A BODY PRESCRIBES. — 3. OF THE FRIENDS OF EQUALITY IN GENERAL.—OMNIPOTENCE OF TRUTH.—IMPORTANCE OF A MILD AND BENEVOLENT PROCEEDING.—CONNECTION BETWEEN LIBERTY AND EQUALITY. — CAUSE OF EQUALITY WILL PERPETUALLY ADVANCE. — SYMPTOMS OF ITS PROGRESS.— IDEA OF ITS FUTURE SUCCESS.— CONCLUSION.

K

HAVING thus stated explicitly and without reserve the great branches of this illustrious
picture, there is but one subject that remains. In
what manner shall this interesting improvement of
human society be carried into execution? Are there
not certain steps that are desirable for this purpose?
Are there not certain steps that are inevitable? Will
not the period that must first elapse, necessarily be
stained with a certain infusion of evil?

No idea has excited greater horror in the minds
of a multitude of persons, than that of the mischiefs that are to ensue from the dissemination of
what they call levelling principles. They believe
" that these principles will inevitably ferment in the
minds of the vulgar, and that the attempt to carry
them into execution will be attended with every
species of calamity." They represent to themselves
" the uninformed and uncivilized part of mankind, as
let loose from all restraint, and hurried into every kind
of excess. Knowledge and taste, the improvements
of intellect, the discoveries of sages, the beauties of
poetry and art, are trampled under foot and extinguished by barbarians. It is another inundation of
Goths and Vandals, with this bitter aggravation, that
the viper that stings us to death was warmed in our
own bosoms."

They conceive of the scene as " beginning in massacre." They suppose " all that is great, pre-eminent

and illustrious as ranking among the first victims. Such as are distinguished by peculiar elegance of manners or energy of diction and composition, will be the inevitable objects of envy and jealousy. Such as intrepidly exert themselves to succour the persecuted, or to declare to the public those truths which they are least inclined, but which are most necessary for them to hear, will be marked out for assassination."

Let us not, from any partiality to the system of equality delineated in this book, shrink from the picture here exhibited. Massacre is the too possible attendant upon revolution, and massacre is perhaps the most hateful scene, allowing for its momentary duration, that any imagination can suggest. The fearful, hopeless expectation of the defeated, and the blood-hound fury of their conquerors, is a complication of mischief that all which has been told of infernal regions cannot surpass. The cold-blooded massacres that are perpetrated under the name of criminal justice fall short of these in their most frightful aggravations. The ministers and instruments of law have by custom reconciled their minds to the dreadful task they perform, and bear their respective parts in the most shocking enormities, without being sensible to the passions allied to those enormities. But the instruments of massacre are actuated with all the sentiments of fiends. Their eyes emit flashes of cruelty and rage. They pursue

their victims from street to street and from house to
house. They tear them from the arms of their fathers
and their wives. They glut themselves with barbarity
and insult, and utter shouts of horrid joy at the spectacle of their tortures.

We have now contemplated the tremendous picture ;
what is the conclusion it behoves us to draw? Must
we shrink from reason, from justice, from virtue and
happiness? Suppose that the inevitable consequence
of communicating truth were the temporary introduction of such a scene as has just been described,
must we on that account refuse to communicate it?
The crimes that were perpetrated would in no just
estimate appear to be the result of truth, but of the
error which had previously been infused. The impartial inquirer would behold them as the last struggles of expiring despotism, which, if it had survived,
would have produced mischiefs, scarcely less atrocious
in the hour of their commission, and infinitely more
calamitous by the length of their duration. If we
would judge truly, even admitting the unfavourable
supposition above stated, we must contrast a moment
of horror and distress with ages of felicity. No
imagination can sufficiently conceive the mental improvement and the tranquil virtue that would succeed,
were property once permitted to rest upon its genuine
basis.

And by what means suppress truth, and keep alive

the salutary intoxication, the tranquillizing insanity
of mind which some men desire? Such has been
too generally the policy of government through every
age of the world. Have we slaves? We must assiduously retain them in ignorance. Have we colonies
and dependencies? The great effort of our care is to
keep them from being too populous and prosperous.
Have we subjects? It is by impotence and misery
that we endeavour to render them supple: plenty is
fit for nothing but to make them unmanageable, dis-
obedient and mutinous. If this were the true philosophy of social institutions, well might we shrink from
it with horror. How tremendous an abortion would
the human species be found, if all that tended to
make them wise, tended to make them unprincipled
and profligate! But this it is impossible for any one
to believe, who will lend the subject a moment's impartial consideration. Can truth, the perception of
justice and a desire to execute it, be the source of
irretrievable ruin to mankind? It may be conceived
that the first opening and illumination of mind will
be attended with disorder. But every just reasoner
must confess that regularity and happiness will succeed to this confusion. To refuse the remedy, were
this picture of its operation ever so true, would be as
if a man who had dislocated a limb, should refuse to
undergo the pain of having it replaced. If mankind
have hitherto lost the road of virtue and happiness,

that can be no just reason why they should be suffered to go wrong for ever. We must not refuse a conviction of error, or even the treading over again some of the steps that were the result of it.

Another question suggests itself under this head. Can we suppress truth? Can we arrest the progress of the inquiring mind? If we can, it will only be done by the most unmitigated despotism. Mind has a perpetual tendency to rise. It cannot be held down but by a power that counteracts its genuine tendency through every moment of its existence. Tyrannical and sanguinary must be the measures employed for this purpose. Miserable and disgustful must be the scene they produce. Their result will be thick darkness of the mind, timidity, servility, hypocrisy. This is the alternative, so far as there is any alternative in their power, between the opposite measures of which the princes and governments of the earth have now to choose: they must either suppress enquiry by the most arbitrary stretches of power, or preserve a clear and tranquil field in which every man shall be at liberty to discover and vindicate his opinion.

No doubt it is the duty of governments to maintain the most unalterable neutrality in this important transaction. No doubt it is the duty of individuals to publish truth without diffidence or reserve, to publish it in its genuine form, without seeking aid from the meretricious arts of publication. The more it is told, the more it is known in its true dimensions, and not in parts, the less is it possible that it should coalesce with or leave room for the pernicious effects of error. The true philanthropist will be eager, instead of suppressing discussion, to take an active share in the scene, to exert the full strength of his faculties in discovery, and to contribute by his exertions to render the operations of thought at once perspicuous and profound.

It being then sufficiently evident that truth must be told at whatever expense, let us proceed to consider the precise amount of that expense, to inquire how much of confusion and violence is inseparable from the transit which mind has to accomplish. And here it plainly appears that mischief is by no means inseparable from the progress. In the mere circumstance of our acquiring knowledge and accumulating one truth after another there is no direct tendency to disorder. Evil can only spring from the clash of mind with mind, from one body of men in the community outstripping another in their ideas of improvement, and becoming impatient of the opposition they have to encounter.

In this interesting period, in which mind shall arrive as it were at the true crisis of its story, there are high duties incumbent upon every branch of the community. First, upon those cultivated and powerful minds, that are fitted to be precursors to the rest in the discovery of truth. They are bound to be active, indefatigable and disinterested. It is incumbent upon them to abstain from inflammatory language, from all expressions of acrimony and resentment. It is absurd in any government to erect itself into a court of criticism in this respect, and to establish a criterion of liberality and decorum; but for that very reason it is doubly incumbent on those who communicate their thoughts to the public, to exercise a rigid censure over themselves. The tidings of liberty and equality are tidings of goodwill to all orders of men. They free the peasant from the iniquity that depresses his mind, and the privileged from the luxury and despotism by which he is corrupted. Let those who bear these tidings not stain their benignity, by showing that that benignity has not yet become the inmate of their hearts.

Nor is it less necessary that they should be urged to tell the whole truth without disguise. No maxim can be more pernicious than that which would teach us to consult the temper of the times, and to tell only so much as we imagine our contemporaries will be able to bear. This practice is at present almost universal, and it is the mark of a very painful degree of depravity. We retail and mangle truth. We impart it to our fellows, not with the liberal measure with which we have received it, but with such parsimony as our own miserable prudence may chance to prescribe. We pretend that truths fit to be practised

in one country, nay, truths which we confess to be
eternally right, are not fit to be practised in another.
That we may deceive others with a tranquil conscience,
we begin with deceiving ourselves. We put shackles
upon our minds, and dare not trust ourselves at large
in the pursuit of truth. This practice took its commencement from the machinations of party, and the
desire of one wise and adventurous leader to carry a
troop of weak, timid and selfish supporters in his train.
There is no reason why I should not declare in any
assembly upon the face of the earth that I am a
republican. There is no more reason why, being a
republican under a monarchical government, I should
enter into a desperate faction to invade the public tranquillity, than if I were monarchical under a republic.
Every community of men, as well as every individual,
must govern itself according to its ideas of justice.
What I should desire is, not by violence to change its
institutions, but by reason to change its ideas. I have
no business with factions or intrigue, but simply to
promulgate the truth, and to wait the tranquil progress
of conviction. If there be any assembly that cannot
bear this, of such an assembly I ought to be no member. It happens much oftener than we are willing to
imagine, that "the post of honour," or, which is better,
the post of utility, " is a private station." [1]

---

[1] Addison's Cato, Act IV. [Godwin's note.]

The dissimulation here censured, beside its ill effects upon him who practises it, and by degrading and unnerving his character upon society at large, has a particular ill consequence with respect to the point we are considering. It lays a mine, and prepares an explosion. This is the tendency of all unnatural restraint. Meanwhile the unfettered progress of truth is always salutary. Its advances are gradual, and each step prepares the general mind for that which is to follow. They are sudden and unprepared emanations of truth, that have the greatest tendency to deprive men of their sobriety and self command. Reserve in this respect is calculated at once to give a rugged and angry tone to the multitude whenever they shall happen to discover what is thus concealed, and to mislead the depositaries of political power. It soothes them into false security, and prompts them to maintain an inauspicious obstinacy.

Having considered what it is that belongs in such a crisis to the enlightened and wise, let us next turn our attention to a very different class of society, the rich and great. And here in the first place it may be remarked, that it is a very false calculation that leads us universally to despair of having these for the advocates of equality. Mankind are not so miserably selfish, as satirists and courtiers have supposed. We never engage in any action without enquiring what is the decision of justice respecting it. We are at all times anxious to satisfy ourselves that what our inclinations lead us to do, is innocent and right to be done. Since therefore justice occupies so large a share in the contemplations of the human mind, it cannot reasonably be doubted that a strong and commanding view of justice would prove a powerful motive to influence our choice. But that virtue which for whatever reason we have chosen, soon becomes recommended to us by a thousand other reasons. We find in it reputation, eminence, self-complacence and the divine pleasures of an approving mind.

The rich and great are far from callous to views of general felicity, when such views are brought before them with that evidence and attraction of which they are susceptible. From one dreadful disadvantage their minds are free. They have not been soured with unrelenting tyranny, or narrowed by the perpetual pressure of distress. They are peculiarly qualified to judge of the emptiness of that pomp and those gratifications, which are always most admired when they are seen from a distance. They will frequently be found considerably indifferent to these things, unless confirmed by habit and rendered inveterate by age. If you show them the attractions of gallantry and magnanimity in resigning them, they will often be resigned without reluctance. Wherever accident of any sort has introduced an active mind, there enterprise is a necessary consequence; and

there are few persons so inactive, as to sit down for
ever in the supine enjoyment of the indulgences to
which they were born. The same spirit that has led
forth the young nobility of successive ages to encounter the hardships of a camp, might easily be
employed to render them champions of the cause of
equality : nor is it to be believed that the circumstance of superior virtue and truth in this latter
exertion will be without its effect.

But let us suppose a considerable party of the rich
and great to be actuated by no view but to their
emolument and ease. It is not difficult to show them,
that their interest in this sense will admit of no more
than a temperate and yielding resistance. Much no
doubt of the future tranquillity or confusion of mankind depends upon the conduct of this party. To
them I would say : " It is in vain for you to fight
against truth. It is like endeavouring with the
human hand to stop the inroad of the ocean. Retire
betimes. Seek your safety in concession. If you
will not go over to the standard of political justice,
temporise at least with an enemy whom you cannot
overcome. Much, inexpressibly much depends upon
you. If you be wise, if you be prudent, if you would
secure at least your lives and your personal ease
amidst the general shipwreck of monopoly and folly,
you will be unwilling to irritate and defy. Unless
by your rashness, there will be no confusion, no

murder, not a drop of blood will be spilt, and you will yourselves be made happy. If you brave the storm and call down every species of odium on your heads, still it is possible, still it is to be hoped that the general tranquillity may be maintained. But, should it prove otherwise, you will have principally to answer for all the consequences that shall ensue.

"Above all, do not be lulled into a rash and headlong security. We have already seen how much the hypocrisy and instability of the wise and enlightened of the present day, those who confess much, and have a confused view of still more, but dare not examine the whole with a steady and unshrinking eye, are calculated to increase this security. But there is a danger still more palpable. Do not be misled by the unthinking and seeming general cry of those who have no fixed principles. Addresses have been found in every age a very uncertain criterion of the future conduct of a people. Do not count upon the numerous train of your adherents, retainers and servants. They afford a very feeble dependence. They are men, and cannot be dead to the interests and claims of mankind. Some of them will adhere to you as long as a sordid interest seems to draw them in that direction. But the moment yours shall appear to be the losing cause, the same interest will carry them over to the enemy's standard. They will disappear like the morning dew.

"May I not hope that you are capable of receiving impression from another argument? Will you feel no compunction at the thought of resisting the greatest of all benefits? Are you content to be regarded by the most enlightened of your contemporaries, and to be handed down to the remotest posterity, as the obstinate adversaries of philanthropy and justice? Can you reconcile it to your own minds, that, for a sordid interest, for the cause of general corruption and abuse, you should be found active in stifling truth, and strangling the new-born happiness of mankind?" Would to God it were possible to carry home this argument to the enlightened and accomplished advocates of aristocracy! Would to God they could be persuaded to consult neither passion, nor prejudice, nor the flights of imagination, in deciding upon so momentous a question! "We know that truth does not stand in need of your alliance to secure her triumph. We do not fear your enmity. But our hearts bleed to see such gallantry, such talents and such virtue enslaved to prejudice, and enlisted in error. It is for your sakes that we expostulate, and for the honour of human nature."

To the general mass of the adherents of the cause of justice it may be proper to say a few words. "If there be any force in the arguments of this work, thus much at least we are authorized to deduce from them, that truth is irresistible. If man be endowed with

a rational nature, then whatever is clearly demon-
strated to his understanding to have the most powerful recommendations, so long as that clearness is
present to his mind, will inevitably engage his choice.
It is to no purpose to say that mind is fluctuating and
fickle; for it is so only in proportion as evidence is
imperfect. Let the evidence be increased, and the
persuasion will be made firmer, and the choice more
uniform. It is the nature of individual mind to be
perpetually adding to the stock of its ideas and knowledge. Similar to this is the nature of general mind,
exclusively of casualties which, arising from a more
comprehensive order of things, appear to disturb the
order of limited systems. This is confirmed to us, if
a truth of this universal nature can derive confirma-
tion from partial experiments, by the regular advances
of the human mind from century to century, since the
invention of printing.

" Let then this axiom of the omnipotence of truth
be the rudder of our undertakings. Let us not pre-
cipitately endeavour to accomplish that to-day, which
the dissemination of truth will make unavoidable to-
morrow. Let us not anxiously watch for occasions
and events : the ascendancy of truth is independent
of events. Let us anxiously refrain from violence :
force is not conviction, and is extremely unworthy of
the cause of justice. Let us admit into our bosoms
neither contempt, animosity, resentment nor revenge.

The cause of justice is the cause of humanity. Its advocates should overflow with universal goodwill. We should love this cause, for it conduces to the general happiness of mankind. We should love it, for there is not a man that lives, who in the natural and tranquil progress of things will not be made happier by its approach. The most powerful cause by which it has been retarded, is the mistake of its adherents, the air of ruggedness, brutishness and inflexibility which they have given to that which in itself is all benignity. Nothing less than this could have prevented the great mass of inquirers from bestowing upon it a patient examination. Be it the care of the now increasing advocates of equality to remove this obstacle to the success of their cause. We have but two plain duties, which, if we set out right, it is not easy to mistake. The first is an unwearied attention to the great instrument of justice, reason. We must divulge our sentiments with the utmost frankness. We must endeavour to impress them upon the minds of others. In this attempt we must give way to no discouragement. We must sharpen our intellectual weapons; add to the stock of our knowledge; be pervaded with a sense of the magnitude of our cause; and perpetually increase that calm presence of mind and self-possession which must enable us to do justice to our principles. Our second duty is tranquillity."

It will not be right to pass over a question that will inevitably suggest itself to the mind of the reader. "If an equalization of property be to take place, not by law, regulation or public institution, but only through the private conviction of individuals, in what manner shall it begin?" In answering this question it is not necessary to prove so simple a proposition, as that all republicanism, all equalization of ranks and immunities, strongly tends towards an equalization of property. Thus, in Sparta this last principle was completely admitted. In Athens the public largesses were so great as almost to exempt the citizens from manual labour; and the rich and eminent only purchased a toleration for their advantages, by the liberal manner in which they opened their stores to the public. In Rome, agrarian laws, a wretched and ill-chosen substitute for equality, but which grew out of the same spirit, were perpetually agitated. If men go on to increase in discernment, and this they certainly will with peculiar rapidity, when the ill-constructed governments which now retard their progress are removed, the same arguments which showed them the injustice of ranks, will show them the injustice of one man's wanting that which, while it is in the possession of another, conduces in no respect to his well being.

It is a common error to imagine, that this injustice will be felt only by the lower orders who suffer from

L

it; and hence it would appear that it can only be corrected by violence. But in answer to this it may, in the first place, be observed that all suffer from it, the rich who engross, as well as the poor who want. Secondly, it has been clearly shown in the course of the present work, that men are not so entirely governed by self interest as has frequently been supposed. It has been shown, if possible, still more clearly, that the selfish are not governed solely by sensual gratification or the love of gain, but that the desire of eminence and distinction is in different degrees an universal passion. Thirdly and principally, the progress of truth is the most powerful of all causes. Nothing can be more absurd than to imagine that theory, in the best sense of the word, is not essentially connected with practice. That which we can be persuaded clearly and distinctly to approve, will inevitably modify our conduct. Mind is not an aggregate of various faculties contending with each other for the mastery, but on the contrary the will is in all cases correspondent to the last judgment of the understanding. When men shall distinctly and habitually perceive the folly of luxury, and when their neighbours are impressed with a similar disdain, it will be impossible that they should pursue the means of it with the same avidity as before.

It will not be difficult perhaps to trace, in the progress of modern Europe from barbarism to refinement, a tendency towards the equalization of property. In the feudal times, as now in India and other parts of the world, men were born to a certain station, and it was nearly impossible for a peasant to rise to the rank of a noble. Except the nobles there were no men that were rich ; for commerce, either external or internal, had scarcely an existence. Commerce was one engine for throwing down this seemingly impregnable barrier, and shocking the prejudices of nobles, who were sufficiently willing to believe that their retainers were a different species of beings from themselves. Learning was another, and more powerful engine. In all ages of the church we see men of the basest origin rising to the highest eminence. Commerce proved that others could rise to wealth beside those who were cased in mail ; but learning proved that the low-born were capable of surpassing their lords. The progressive effect of these ideas may easily be traced by the attentive observer. Long after learning began to unfold its powers, its votaries still submitted to those obsequious manners and servile dedications, which no man reviews at the present day without astonishment. It is but lately that men have known that intellectual excellence can accomplish its purposes without a patron. At present, among the civilized and well informed a man of slender wealth, but of great intellectual powers and a firm and virtuous mind, is constantly received with

attention and deference; and his purse-proud neighbour who should attempt to treat him superciliously,
is sure to be discountenanced in his usurpation. The
inhabitants of distant villages, where long-established
prejudices are slowly destroyed, would be astonished
to see how comparatively small a share wealth has in
determining the degree of attention with which men
are treated in enlightened circles.

These no doubt are but slight indications. It is
with morality in this respect as it is with politics.
The progress is at first so slow as for the most part
to elude the observation of mankind; nor can it
indeed be adequately perceived but by the contempla-
tion and comparison of events during a considerable
portion of time. After a certain interval, the scene
is more fully unfolded, and the advances appear more
rapid and decisive. While wealth was everything,
it was to be expected that men would acquire it,
though at the expense of character and integrity.
Absolute and universal truth had not yet shown
itself so decidedly, as to be able to enter the lists
with what dazzled the eye or gratified the sense.
In proportion as the monopolies of rank and com-
panies are abolished, the value of superfluities will
not fail to decline. In proportion as republicanism
gains ground, men will come to be estimated for
what they are, not for what force has given, and force
may take away.

Let us reflect for a moment on the gradual consequences of this revolution of opinion. Liberality of
dealing will be among its earliest results, and of consequence accumulation will become less frequent and
less enormous. Men will not be disposed, as now,
to take advantage of each other's distresses, and to
demand a price for their aid, not measured by a
general standard, but by the wants of an individual.
They will not consider how much they can extort, but
how much it is reasonable to require. The master
tradesman who employs labourers under him, will be
disposed to give a more ample reward to their industry, which he is at present enabled to tax chiefly
by the neutral circumstance of having provided a
capital. Liberality on the part of his employer will
complete in the mind of the artisan, what ideas of
political justice will probably have begun. He will
no longer spend the little surplus of his earnings in
that dissipation, which is at present one of the principal causes that subject him to the arbitrary pleasure
of a superior. He will escape from the irresolution
of slavery and the fetters of despair, and perceive that
independence and ease are scarcely less within his
reach than that of any other member of the community. This is a natural step towards the still
further progression, in which the labourer will receive
entire whatever the consumer may be required to pay,
without having a middle man, an idle and useless

monopolizer, as he will then be found, to fatten upon
his spoils.

The same sentiments that lead to liberality of dealing, will also lead to liberality of distribution. The
trader, who is unwilling to grow rich by extorting
from his employer or his workmen, will also refuse to
become rich by the not inferior injustice of withhold-
ing from his poor neighbour the supply he wants.
The habit which was created in the former case of
being contented with moderate gains, is closely connected with the habit of being contented with slender
accumulation. He that is not anxious to add to his
heap, will not be reluctant by a benevolent distribution to prevent its increase. Wealth was once almost
the single object of pursuit that presented itself to
the gross and uncultivated mind. Various objects
will hereafter divide men's attention, the love of
liberty, the love of equality, the pursuits of art and
the desire of knowledge. These objects will not, as
now, be confined to a few, but will gradually be laid
open to all. The love of liberty obviously leads to
the love of man : the sentiment of benevolence will
be increased, and the narrowness of the selfish affections will decline. The general diffusion of truth will
be productive of general improvement ; and men will
daily approximate towards those views according to
which every object will be appreciated at its true
value. Add to which, that the improvement of which

we speak is general, not individual. The progress
is the progress of all. Each man will find his sentiments of justice and rectitude echoed, encouraged and
strengthened by the sentiments of his neighbours.
Apostasy will be made eminently improbable, because
the apostate will incur, not only his own censure, but
the censure of every beholder.

One remark will suggest itself upon these considerations. " If the inevitable progress of improvement insensibly lead towards an equalization of
property, what need was there of proposing it as a
specific object to men's consideration ? " The answer
to this objection is easy. The improvement in question consists in a knowledge of truth. But our knowledge will be very imperfect so long as this great
branch of universal justice fails to constitute a part
of it. All truth is useful ; can this truth, which is
perhaps more fundamental than any, be without its
benefits ? Whatever be the object towards which
mind spontaneously advances, it is of no mean importance to us to have a distinct view of that object. Our
advances will thus become accelerated. It is a well-
known principle of morality, that he who proposes
perfection to himself, though he will inevitably fall
short of what he pursues, will make a more rapid
progress, than he who is contented to aim only at
what is imperfect. The benefits to be derived in the
interval from a view of equalization, as one of the

great objects towards which we are tending, are exceedingly conspicuous. Such a view will strongly conduce to make us disinterested now. It will teach us to look with contempt upon mercantile speculations, commercial prosperity, and the cares of gain. It will impress us with a just apprehension of what it is of which man is capable and in which his perfection consists; and will fix our ambition and activity upon the worthiest objects. Mind cannot arrive at any great and illustrious attainment, however much the nature of mind may carry us towards it, without feeling some presages of its approach; and it is reasonable to believe that, the earlier these presages are introduced, and the more distinct they are made, the more auspicious will be the event.

INDEX.

www.ingramcontent.com/pod-product-compliance
Lightning Source LLC
Chambersburg PA
CBHW020556270326
41927CB00006B/862